Tasty Knits

Made with Love

First published in Great Britain 2011

Search Press Limited
Wellwood, North Farm Road,
Tunbridge Wells, Kent TN2 3DR

Based on the following books published by Search Press:
Twenty to Make: Knitted Fast Food by Susie Johns (2010)
Twenty to Make: Knitted Fruit by Susie Johns (2010)
Twenty to Make: Knitted Vegetables by Susie Johns (2010)
Twenty to Make: Knitted Cakes by Susan Penny (2008)

Photographs by Debbie Patterson at Search Press Studios (pages 1, 3, 4, 8–57 and 96)
and Roddy Paine Photographic Studio (pages 2, 5, 9, 58–96)

ISBN: 978-1-84448-666-3

Suppliers
If you have difficulty in obtaining any of the materials and equipment mentioned in
this book, then please visit the Search Press website for details of suppliers:
www.searchpress.com

Printed in China.

Tasty Knits

Made with Love

Susan Penny
and Susie Johns

Search Press

Contents

Introduction

In our fast-paced world, delicious food is everywhere. From burger joints and hot-dog stands, market stalls and food courts, delicatessens and bakeries, we are offered instant gratification in the form of ready-to-eat cupcakes, pies and pastries, sandwiches, samosas, noodles and sweet treats – some familiar, some exotic and some more nutritious than others but all very tasty and tempting.

The knitted cakes, snacks, fruit and fast food in this book are aimed at all ages and abilities and make good gifts; most are designed as 'play food' and are suitable for children as long as you do not add any beads and you sew components together very securely (the pointed wooden skewers should be removed from the kebabs and so should the wooden lollipop sticks).

If you want to start with something simple, try the fried egg or Swiss roll. More confident knitters will enjoy making the slices of fruit pie and wedding cake, while those who like patterns that require you to knit in the round on double-pointed needles may like to try the hamburger or ice cream.

They are all fun to make and a great way to use up oddments of yarn left over from larger projects. However, the modern wool shop has shelves replete with a sea of colours and textures – sensuous mohair next to natural organic cotton, and fun, funky polyester next to soft merino. The projects in this book use many of these wonderful yarns, so do not feel afraid to try one of those gorgeous wools you have had your eye on. Whatever you choose to knit, have fun!

Opposite:

Here is a feast for the eyes! With pasties, pitta pockets, pizza, sandwiches, burgers, prawns, noodles and kebabs, you can knit your own banquet.

6

Knitting notes

Most of the items in this book are made from double knitting yarn. While in some cases suggestions are given for certain yarn compositions – wool, acrylic, and blends containing cashmere, silk, bamboo or alpaca, for example – you should feel free to experiment with the yarns you have available to you. If you need to buy only a small amount of a certain colour, a skein of tapestry yarn may suffice. In a few cases, novelty textured yarns have been used to produce certain effects, such as the seeds in a slice of wholegrain bread.

Unless otherwise stated, right and wrong sides of work are often interchangeable: just decide which side looks best. Tension (or gauge) are not given: just aim for a firm, close-knit fabric that will hold its shape and not allow the stuffing to poke through, using a larger or smaller needle than the one stated in the pattern, if necessary, to produce the desired effect.

Abbreviations

beg: begin(ning)

dec: decrease (by working two stitches together)

DK: double knitting

g st: garter stitch (knit every row)

inc: increase (by working into the front and back of the stitch)

inc1: knit into front and back of same stitch

inc 2: knit into front, back and front of stitch

k: knit

k2tog: knit two stitches together

M1: make one stitch

p: purl

psso: pass the slipped stitch over

p2tog: purl two stitches together

rib: ribbing (one stitch knit, one stitch purl)

rem: remain(ing)

rep: repeat(ing)

sl1: slip one stitch on to the right-hand needle without knitting it

st(s): stitch(es)

st st: stocking stitch (one row knit, one row purl)

tbl: through back loop

yfwd: yarn forward

yon: yarn over needle

Materials:

3 balls DK yarn – 1 beige, 1 ivory and 1 leaf green

1 ball felting yarn – brown

1 ball silk or rayon yarn – yellow

Polyester fibrefill

Craft foam, 2mm (1⁄16in) thick

Tapestry needle

Needles:

1 pair 3.00mm (UK 11; US 2) knitting needles

1 pair 3.75mm (UK 9; US 5) knitting needles

Set of four double-pointed 3.00mm (UK 11; US 2) knitting needles

Instructions:

Meat patty (make 1)

With double-pointed 3.00mm (UK 11; US 2) knitting needles and brown felting yarn, cast on 12 sts and divide equally between three needles.

Round 1: k to end.

Round 2: (k1, inc 1 in next st) 6 times [18 sts].

Round 3: k to end.

Round 4: (k2, inc 1 in next st) 6 times [24 sts].

Round 5: k to end.

Round 6: (k3, inc 1 in next st) 6 times [30 sts].

Round 7: k to end.

Round 8: (k4, inc 1 in next st) 6 times [36 sts].

Round 9: k to end.

Round 10: (k5, inc 1 in next st) 6 times [42 sts].

Round 11: k to end.

Round 12: (k6, inc 1 in next st) 6 times [48 sts].

Round 13: k to end.

Round 14: (k7, inc 1 in next st) 6 times [54 sts].

Rounds 15–16: k to end.

Round 17: (k7, k2tog) 6 times [48 sts].

Round 18: k to end.

Round 19: (k6, k2tog) 6 times [42 sts].

Round 20: k to end.

Round 21: (k5, k2tog) 6 times [36 sts].

Round 22: k to end.

Round 23: (k4, k2tog) 6 times [30 sts].

Round 24: k to end.

Round 25: (k3, k2tog) 6 times [24 sts].

Round 26: k to end.

Round 27: (k2, k2tog) 6 times [18 sts].

Round 28: k to end.

Round 29: (k1, k2tog) 6 times [12 sts].

Round 30: k to end.

Round 31: (k2tog) 6 times [6 sts].

Break yarn and thread through rem sts.

Bun (make 2)

With double-pointed 3.00mm (UK 11; US 2) knitting needles and beige double knitting yarn, cast on 12 sts and divide equally between three needles.

Work as for meat patty to Round 15.

Round 16: (k8, inc 1 in next st) 6 times [60 sts].

Round 17: k.

Round 18: (k9, inc 1 in next st) 6 times [66 sts].

Rounds 19-22: k.

Break yarn and join in ivory double knitting yarn.

Rounds 23–24: k.

Round 25: (k9, k2tog) 6 times [60 sts].

Round 26: (k8, k2tog) 6 times [54 sts].

Round 27: (k7, k2tog) 6 times [48 sts].

Round 28: (k6, k2tog) 6 times [42 sts].

Round 29: (k5, k2tog) 6 times [36 sts].

Round 30: (k4, k2tog) 6 times [30 sts].

Round 31: (k3, k2tog) 6 times [24 sts].

Round 32: (k2, k2tog) 6 times [18 sts].

Round 33: (k1, k2tog) 6 times [12 sts].

Round 34: (k2tog) 6 times [6 sts].

Break yarn and thread through rem sts.

Lettuce (make 1)

With size 3.75mm (UK 9; US 5) needles and green double knitting yarn, cast on 14 sts.
Row 1: inc in each st to end [28 sts].
Row 3: (inc 1, k1) to end [42 sts].
Row 4: (inc 1, k2) to end [56 sts].
Row 5: (inc 1, k3) to end [70 sts].
Row 6: (inc 1, k4) to end [84 sts].
Rows 7–13: Starting with a knit row, work st st.
Row 14: k to end.
Cast off; break yarn, leaving long tail.

Mustard (make 1)

With yellow silk or rayon yarn and size 3.00mm (UK 11; US 2) needles, cast on 3 sts.
Row 1: k to end.
Row 2: p to end.
Row 3: inc 1, k1, inc 1 [5 sts].
Rows 4–20: Starting with a purl row, work st st.
Row 21: k2tog, k1, k2tog [3 sts].
Row 23: p to end.
Row 24: k to end.
Cast off; break yarn, leaving long tail.

Making up

For a thin burger, cut one or two circles of craft foam and slip them both inside, then pull up the thread and fasten off to close the holes on the top and base. Pull up the yarn on the last round of the bun and fasten off to close the hole on the 'cut' side of the bun. Stuff the bun with polyester fibrefill through the hole in the top, then neatly stitch the opening closed.

Join the two short edges of the lettuce leaf using the tail of yarn. Join the two side edges of the mustard, then weave in all yarn ends.

You can keep the components separate or stitch them together, sandwiching the meat patty with the lettuce between two buns. The finished bun measures 8.5cm (3⅜in) across.

Can I Have a Cheeseburger, Please?
To add a sprinkling of sesame seeds to the top of the bun, thread a tapestry needle with ivory yarn and make a series of small single stitches in a random pattern. To make the cheese, use size 3.75mm (UK 9; US 5) needles and yellow cotton yarn. Cast on 18 sts and work 30 rows in g st (knit every row), then cast off.

Cheese Sandwich

Materials:

2 balls acrylic or wool DK flecked yarn –
    1 light beige and 1 beige

1 ball bamboo blend DK yarn – yellow

Craft foam, 2mm (1/16in) thick

Polyester fibrefill

Tapestry needle and thread

Needles:

1 pair 3.00mm (UK 11; US 2) knitting needles

1 pair 4.00mm (UK 8; US 6) knitting needles

Instructions:

Bread (make 4)

With size 3.00mm (UK 11; US 2)
needles, cast on 20 sts in light
beige yarn.
Rows 1–34: k to end.
Rows 35–36: inc 1, k to last st, inc 1
[24 sts].
Rows 37–40: g st.
Row 41: dec 1, k to last 2 sts, k tog [22 sts].
Row 42: k to end.
Rows 43 and 44: as row 41 [18 sts].
Cast off.

Crust (make 2)

With size 3.00mm (UK 11; US 2) needles, cast on
4 sts in beige yarn.
Row 1: sl1, k3.
Rep row 1 until work measures 38cm (15in) or is the right length to
fit around the edges of the bread slice.
Cast off.

Cheese (make 1)

With size 4.00mm (UK 8; US 6) needles, cast on 16sts in yellow yarn.
Row 1: sl1, k to end.
Rows 2–33: Rep row 1.
Cast off.

Making up

Using the finished bread as a template, cut two pieces of craft foam. To
make up one slice of bread, arrange a thin layer of polyester fibrefill on the
wrong side of one bread piece, top it with craft foam, add a few more wisps
of polyester fibrefill, then top with a second piece of bread.

Pin and stitch a crust all round and oversew the edges of the crust to
each bread piece. Repeat for a second slice of bread. Place the cheese in
between the two slices of bread and secure with a few stitches, if you wish.

The finished sandwich measures approximately 12cm (4¾in) long, 11cm
(4½in) wide and 5cm (2in) thick.

Lunch Break

Fast food does not have to be junk food. A heathy wholegrain sandwich is quick to prepare even when it is this knitted version. For a white bread sandwich, knit the bread slices in white or off-white. To make a slice of ham, follow the instructions for the cheese but use yarn in a suitable shade of pink.

Pizza Slice

Materials:

5 balls DK yarn – 1 beige, 1 red, 1 dark red, 1 green, 1 off-white

1 ball cotton DK yarn – white

1 ball 4-ply silk yarn – yellow

1 ball 4-ply cotton yarn – coral

Tapestry needle

Instructions:

Base (make 1)

With size 3.75mm (UK 9; US 5) needles and beige yarn, cast on 1 st.
Row 1: k into front, back and front of st [3 sts].
*Row 2: sl1, k to end.
Rows 3–4: Rep row 2.
Row 5: inc 1, k to last st, inc 1.**
Rep from * to ** until there are 31 sts.
Next row: cast off 3 sts, k to end [28 sts].
Next row: cast off 3 sts, k to end [25 sts].
Next row: cast off 4 sts, k to end [21 sts].
Next row: cast off 4 sts, k to end [17 sts].
Next row: cast off 5 sts, k to end [12 sts].
Next row: cast off 5 sts, k to end [7 sts].
Cast off rem 7 sts.

Crust (make 1)

With two 3.75mm (UK 9; US 5) double-pointed needles and beige yarn, cast on 3 sts.
Row 1: k3; do not turn but slide sts to other end of needle.
Rep row 1 until cord is long enough to fit around outer edge of crust.

Needles:

1 pair 3.75mm (UK 9; US 5) knitting needles

1 pair 3.00mm (UK 11; US 2) knitting needles

1 pair of 4.50mm (UK 7; US 7) knitting needles

Two double-pointed 3.75mm (UK 9; US 5) knitting needles

Tomato sauce (make 1)

With size 4.50mm (UK 7; US 7) needles and red yarn, cast on 1 st.
Row 1: k into front, back and front of st [3 sts].
Continue as for base, rep instructions from * to ** until there are 19 sts.
Next row: k2tog, k3, inc 1, k3, sl1, k2tog, psso, k3, inc 1, k1, k2tog [17 sts].
Next row: k2tog, k2, inc 1, k2, sl1, k2tog, psso, k2, inc 1, k2, k2tog [15 sts].
Next row: k7, turn and cast off; break yarn.
Rejoin yarn to rem 8 sts, k to end, then cast off.

Cheese (make 2)

With size 4.50mm (UK 7; US 7) needles and yellow yarn, cast on 9 sts.
Rows 1–11: g st (knit every row).

Pepperoni (make 6)

With size 3.00mm (UK11; US 2) needles and coral yarn, cast on 3sts.
Row 1: inc in each st to end [6 sts].
Row 2: k to end.
Row 3: inc in each st to end [12 sts].
Row 4: inc in each st to end [24 sts].
Cast off.
Stitch row ends together, to form a disc.
Thread tapestry needle with length of dark red yarn and work blanket stitch around perimeter, stitch by stitch, on cast-off row..

Pepper slice (make 3)

With size 3.00mm (UK11; US 2) needles and green yarn, cast on 12 sts.
Row 1: k2tog tbl 6 times.
Cast off.

Mushroom (make 4)

With size 3.75mm (UK 9; US 5) needles and white yarn, cast on 4 sts.
Rows 1–4: g st (knit every row).

Row 5: k1, (inc 1) twice, k1 [6 sts].
Row 6: inc in each st to end [8 sts].
Cast off.

Making up

Stitch the crust to the curved edge of the base. Stitch the tomato sauce on to the base.

If desired, thread the tapestry needle with green yarn and work a scattering of small stitches all over the tomato sauce, like flecks of herbs.

Next, choose your toppings. To stitch the pepperoni in place, use off-white yarn and small stitches to represent flecks of fat. For all of the other toppings, use matching yarns to stitch them in place, trying to make the stitches as discreet as possible.

Just Like Mamma Used To Make
Here one slice is topped with pepperoni while the other combines mushrooms, cheese and green peppers. The finished pizza slice, with topping, measures approximately 15cm (6in) long, 14cm (5½in) wide and 1cm (⅜in) thick.

Bacon and Egg

Materials:

2 balls wool or cashmere blend DK yarn –
1 ivory and 1 yellow

1 ball 4-ply cotton yarn – brick red

Polyester fibrefill

Tapestry needle and thread

1 button, 3cm (1⅛in) diameter

Instructions:

Bacon (make 2)

Begin by making the rind. With 3.00mm (UK 10; US 3) double-pointed needles and ivory, cast on 3 sts.

Row 1: k3; do not turn but slide sts to other end of needle.

Rows 2–62: Rep row 1; then cast off, but do not break yarn.

Row 63: Using same yarn and needles, pick up and k 41 sts (including st already on needle after casting off), evenly spaced, along the length of the cord; do not break yarn.

Rows 64–65: Join in brick red yarn and work in g st; do not break yarn.

Row 66: (RS) With ivory yarn, k to end; do not break yarn but slide the sts to the other end of the needle.

Row 67: (RS) With brick red yarn, k to end.

Row 68: (WS) With ivory yarn, p to end; do not break yarn but slide the sts to the other end of the needle.

Row 69: (WS) With brick red yarn, p to end.

Row 70: (RS): With ivory yarn, k to end; break yarn and slide sts to the other end of the needle.

Rows 71–73: (RS) With brick red yarn, and starting with a p row, work st st.

Cast off.

Egg white (make 1)

With 3.25mm (UK 10; US 3) needles and ivory or white yarn, cast on 8 sts.

Row 1: k to end.

Row 2: p to end.

Rows 3–10: Cont in st st, inc 1 st at each end of next 6 rows and then 1 st at each end of next 2 alt rows [24 sts].

Needles:

1 pair 3.25mm (UK 10; US 3) knitting needles

Two double-pointed 3.00mm (UK 11; US 2) knitting needles

Rows 11–24: Work 14 rows in st st without further shaping.

Row 25: (RS) k2tog, k to last 2 sts, k2tog.

Row 26: p to end.

Rows 27–28: Rep last two rows once more. [20 sts].

Rows 29–34: Cont in st st, dec 1 st at each end of next 6 rows [8 sts].

Row 35: k to end.

Row 36: p to end.

Cast off.

Egg yolk (make 1)

With size 3.25mm (UK 10; US 3) needles and yellow yarn, cast on 6 sts.

Row 1: k to end.

Row 2: inc 1, k to end.

Rows 3–11: Rep row 2 [16 sts].

Rows 12–23: g st.

Row 24: k2tog, k to end [15 sts].

Rows 25–33: Rep row 24 [6 sts].

Cast off, leaving a tail of yarn.

Making up

Thread a tapestry needle with the tail of yarn from the egg yolk and run a gathering stitch all round the edge. Place the button inside, with a few wisps of polyester fibrefill for extra padding, then pull up the yarn end tightly to gather up and enclose the button.

Secure it with a few stitches, then stitch it to the egg white. The finished bacon rashers are approximately 18cm (7in) long and 3.5cm (1⅜in) wide, while the egg measures approximately 12cm (4¾in) in diameter.

Full English Breakfast

Here we have the great British breakfast, delicious and satisfying. It takes no time at all, with yarn and needles, to create a couple of crisp rashers and a perfect fried egg – free range, of course! Why not make a sausage (see instructions on page 18) to add to the egg and bacon, and turn your breakfast into a real slap-up meal?

Hot Dog

Materials:

3 balls wool DK yarn – 1 brown, 1 beige and 1 ivory

1 ball 4-ply silk or rayon yarn – yellow

Polyester fibrefill

Tapestry needle

Needles:

1 pair 3.00mm (UK 11; US 2) knitting needles

Set of four 3.00mm (UK 11; US 2) double-pointed
 knitting needles

Instructions:

Frankfurter (make 1)

With the set of four size 3.00mm (UK 11;
US 2) needles and brown double knitting yarn,
cast on 18 sts and divide equally between three
needles.

Knit 60 rounds.

Break yarn and thread through each stitch.

Bread roll:

Crust (make 2)

With size 3.00mm (UK 11; US 2) needles, cast
on 6 sts in beige yarn.

Row 1: inc1, k1, (inc 1) twice, k1, inc1 [10 sts].

Row 2: inc, k3, (inc 1) twice, k3, inc1 [14 sts].

Row 3: k6, (inc 1) twice, k6 [16 sts].

Row 4: k.

Row 5: k7, (inc 1) twice, k7 [18 sts].

Rows 6–61: g st.

Row 62: k7, (k2tog) twice, k7 [16 sts].

Row 63: k.

Row 64: k6, (k2tog) twice, k6 [14 sts].

Row 65: k2tog, k3, (k2tog) twice, k3,
k2tog [10 sts].

Row 66: k2tog, k1, (k2tog) twice, k1,
k2tog [6 sts].

Row 67: k to end.

Cast off.

Bread (make 2)

With 3.00mm (UK 11; US 2) needles, cast on 5
sts in ivory yarn.

Row 1: k1, (inc 1, k1) twice [7 sts].

Row 2 and each even-numbered row: k.

Row 3: k1, inc 1, k3, inc 1, k1 [9 sts].

Row 5: k1, inc 1, k5, inc 1, k1 [11 sts].

Row 7: k1, inc 1, k7, inc 1, k1 [13 sts].

Rows 8–54: g st.

Row 55: k1, k2tog, k7, k2tog, k1 [11 sts].

Row 57: k1, k2tog, k5, k2tog, k1 [9 sts].

Row 59: k1, k2tog, k3, k2tog, k1 [7 sts].

Row 61: k1, (k2tog, k1) twice [5 sts].

Cast off.

Mustard (make 1)

With two 3.00mm (UK 11; US 2) double-pointed
needles, cast on 3 sts in yellow yarn.

Row 1: k3; do not turn but slide sts to other
end of needle.

Rep this row until work measures 20cm (7¾in);
fasten off.

Making up

Pull up the yarn on the last round of the
sausage and fasten it off to close the hole. Stuff
the sausage through the cast-on edge, then
neatly stitch the opening closed.

   Thread matching yarn through each end of
the bread roll crust and pull up very slightly
to gather, then stitch the bread to the crust,
leaving a small opening; stuff and stitch
opening closed. Stitch the bread rolls together
along one long edge, leaving the other edge
open. Stitch the mustard to the frankfurter,
bending it into a wiggly line as you go. You can
either stitch the frankfurter in place or, if it is
intended as part of a play food set, leave the
two items separate.

   The finished frankfurter measures 16cm
(6¼in) in length; the bread roll measures
15cm (6in).

Sausages

Plump and inviting, who could resist this delicious frankfurter nestling within a soft bread roll with a tantalising wiggle of mustard? For a hearty British breakfast, knit a sausage to accompany the egg and bacon on page 17. Follow the method for the frankfurter but use brown double knitting yarn, cast on only 12 stitches and work only 50 rounds.

Pitta Pocket

Materials:

5 balls wool DK yarn – 1 beige, 1 light beige, 1 leaf green, 1 white and 1 pink

Polyester fibrefill

Tapestry needle

Needles:

1 pair 3.00mm (UK 11; US 2) knitting needles

Instructions:

Pitta bread (make 1)

With size 3.00mm (UK 11; US 2) needles, cast on 7 sts in beige yarn.
*Row 1: k.
Row 2: cast on 2, k to end.
Rows 3–5: Rep row 2 [15 sts].
Row 6: inc 1, k to end.
Rows 7–15: Rep row 6 [25 sts]*.
Rows 16–55: g st.
**Row 56: k2tog, k to end.
Rows 57–65: Rep row 56 [15 sts].
Row 66: cast off 2, k to end.
Rows 67–69: Rep row 66 [7 sts]**.
Rep from Row 1 once more.
Cast off.

Chicken (make 5)

With size 3.00mm (UK 11; US 2) needles, cast on 11 sts in light beige yarn.
Row 1: k5, p1, k5.
Row 2: p5, k1, p5.
Row 3: k5, p1, k5.
Row 4: p5, k1, p5.
Row 5: k2tog, k3, p1, k3, k2tog [9 sts].
Row 6: p4, k1, p4.
Row 7: k4, p1, k4.
Row 8: p4, k1, p4.
Row 9: k2tog, k2, p1, k2, k2tog [7 sts].
Row 10: p3, k1, p3.
Row 11: k3, p1, k3.
Row 12: p3, k1, p3.
Row 13: k2tog, k1, p1, k1, k2tog [5 sts].
Row 14: p2, k1, p2.
Row 15: k2, p1, k2.
Row 16: p2, k1, p2.
Cast off.

Lettuce strip (make 9)

With size 3.00mm (UK 11; US 2) needles, cast on 15 sts in leaf green yarn.
Row 1: (inc 1, k1) 7 times, inc 1 [23 sts].
Cast off.

Onion ring (make 3 pink and 2 white)

With size 3.00mm (UK 11; US 2) needles and pink yarn, cast on 38 sts using the cable method; break yarn.
With white yarn, k2tog tbl 19 times. Cast off.
For white onion, use white yarn throughout.

Making up

Fold the pitta bread in half along the 'hinge', with right sides together, and stitch the edges together with backstitch, leaving one long edge open. Fold 3mm (⅛in) to the inside along the opening and slip stitch to form a neat hem before turning right sides out. Fold each chicken piece in half with the purl side outwards and oversew the sides together (adding a tiny amount of stuffing, if you wish). Join the ends of each onion ring strip to form a ring.

Knitting notes

When sewing up the chicken pieces, there is no need to be too neat, as uneven stitches will help to create a more lopsided, authentic look. To stuff the chicken pieces, instead of polyester stuffing, use short lengths of yarn salvaged after weaving in ends, as they will create a more lumpy appearance.

The finished pitta pocket measures approximately 17cm (6¾in) long and 11cm (4¼in) wide.

Half Pitta

A Middle Eastern flat bread is cut open and filled with crisp lettuce and slivers of chicken – but you can vary the filling according to your taste. Make as many pieces of chicken, lettuce strips and onion rings as you wish.

For the not-so-hungry, half a pitta bread will suffice. Using the same yarn and needles, cast on 25 sts and work 25 rows, then follow the pattern from ** to ** then from * to * and work a further 25 rows without shaping before casting off. Stitch side seams and turn under a 3mm (⅛in) hem on the open edge, as before.

Sushi

Materials:

4 balls wool DK yarn – 1 red or orange, 1 green,
   1 yellow and 1 coral

1 ball 4-ply silk or rayon yarn – ivory

Polyester fibrefill

Black rayon or satin ribbon, 24mm (1in) wide

Sewing needle and black thread

Tapestry needle

Needles:

1 pair 3.00mm (UK 11; US 2) knitting needles

Instructions:

Maki (made in one piece)

With size 3.00mm (UK 11; US 2) needles and
red or orange DK yarn, cast on 5 sts.
Row 1–8: Starting with a k row, work st st.
Rows 9–20: Break yarn and join in green yarn.
Work a further 12 rows in st st.
Row 21: Change to ivory yarn, used double.
(k1, p1) to end of row.
Rows 22–65: Rep row 21.
Cast off, leaving a tail of yarn for stitching.

Uramaki filling

With size 3.00mm (UK 11; US 2) needles and
yellow yarn, cast on 5 sts.
Rows 1–12: k. Cast off.

Uramaki rice

With size 3.00mm (UK 11; US 2) needles and
ivory yarn, used double, cast on 6 sts.
Row 1: (k1, p1) to end of row.
Rows 2–72: Rep row 1.
Cast off, leaving a tail of yarn for stitching.

Nigiri rice

With size 3.00mm (UK 11; US 2) needles and
ivory yarn, cast on 3 sts.
*Row 1: p1, k1, p1.
Row 2: as row 1.
Row 3: inc 1, k1, inc 1 [5 sts].
Row 4: k1, (p1, k1) twice.
Rows 5–22: Rep row 4.
Row 23: k2tog, k1, k2tog [3 sts].**
Rep from * to ** twice more.
Next row: p1, k1, p1.
Cast off, leaving a tail of yarn for stitching.

Maki

Uramaki

Nigiri

Nigiri topping

With size 3.00mm (UK 11; US 2) needles and
yellow or coral yarn, cast on 3 sts.
Row 1: p3.
Row 2: inc 1, k1, inc 1 [5 sts].
Rows 3–21: Starting with a p row, work st st.
Row 22: k2tog, k1, k2tog [3 sts]. Cast off.

Making up

For maki, roll up the strip, starting with the
cast-on edge, and stitch the cast-off edge to
the roll, using the tail of yarn to stop it from
unrolling. Then cut a piece of ribbon long
enough to go round the outside of the roll
with an extra 4mm (⅛in) for overlap. With black
thread, stitch one end of the ribbon to the roll,
wrap around, fold under the remaining end
and stitch it neatly in place over the first end.

For uramaki, roll up the filling and secure it
with one or two stitches. Cut a piece of ribbon
long enough to encase the filling with an extra
4mm (⅛in) for overlap, wrap around, fold under
the remaining end and stitch neatly in place
using black thread. Secure one end of the rice
strip to the ribbon, then continue rolling. Once
finished, stitch the cast-off edge to the roll,
using the tail of yarn.

For nigiri, fold the rice in three, forming
a three-layered piece, and stitch the sides
together, adding a few wisps of stuffing
between layers, if necessary. Secure the
topping in place with a few stitches. Cut a
10cm (4in) length of ribbon, fold in the edges
to form a narrow strip, then wrap it around the
roll and stitch the ends together underneath.

Sushi

As good to look at as it is to eat, a plate of sushi is a visual delight. Here, silky yarn represents rice while ribbon 'seaweed' encases each delicious morsel. Maki (the ribbon-covered round pieces) and uramaki (the white round pieces) are 3cm (1⅛in) in diameter; while nigiri (the long ribbon-wrapped pieces) are each 7cm (2¾in) long.

Cornish Pasty

Materials:

2 balls DK yarn – 1 beige and 1 leaf green

Polyester fibrefill

Tapestry needle

Needles:

1 pair 3.00mm (UK 11; US 2) knitting needles

Two double-pointed 3.00mm (UK 11; US 2) knitting needles

Instructions:

Pastry (make 1)

With size 3.00mm (UK 11; US 2) needles and beige yarn, cast on 14 sts.
Row 1 (RS): p to end.
Row 2: inc 1, k to last st, inc 1 [16 sts].
Rows 3–16: Rep rows 1 and 2 [30 sts].
Rows 17–23: Starting with a p row, work st st without further shaping.
Row 24: k2tog, k to last 2 sts, k2tog [28 sts].
Row 25: p to end.
Rows 26–39: Rep last 2 rows [14 sts].
Cast off.

Crimp (make 1)

With size 3.00mm (UK 11; US 2) double-pointed needles and beige yarn, cast on 4 sts.
Row 1: k4; do not turn but slide sts to other end of needle.
Rep this row until work measures 30cm (12in); fasten off, leaving tail of yarn for sewing.

Parsley stem (make 1)

With size 3.00mm (UK 11; US 2) double-pointed needles and green yarn, cast on 2 sts.
Row 1: k2; do not turn but slide sts to other end of needle.
Rep this row until work measures 3cm (1⅛in) in length.

Parsley leaves

*Next row: inc 2 in each st [4 sts].
Next row: inc 2 in each st [8 sts].**
Cast off but do not break yarn.
There is one st on needle; pick up 1 st from end of cord, at base of leaves you have just made, and rep from * to ** once more.
Cast off, leaving a tail of yarn.

Making up

Fold the pastry in half, with the RS (purl side) outwards and stitch the edges together using the tapestry needle and spare yarn, leaving a small gap. Insert stuffing through the gap, then close it with a few more stitches. Thread the tail of yarn at the end of the cord on to the tapestry needle and gather the cord by passing the needle right through, from side to side in a zigzag motion, on every fourth row, then pull up until the crimped cord fits around the seam of the pasty. Stitch it in place.

Use the tail of yarn to secure the ends of the parsley leaves to top of stalk, encouraging the leaves to form clusters as you do so.

The finished pasty measures approximately 13cm (5in) long, 5cm (2in) wide and 3cm (1⅛in) deep.

Pasty and Empanada

A savoury filling encased in a circle of pastry, folded and crimped, was the snack of choice for Cornish miners – and you will find variations on this theme all round the world.

To make an empanada, a Spanish and South American version, use a paler coloured yarn and make up with the knit side outwards. Make a cord just long enough to fit along the seam, without gathering, and stitch it in place.

Meat Pie

Materials:

1 ball DK yarn – beige

Polyester fibrefill

Tapestry needle

Craft foam, 1cm (⅜in) thick

Instructions:

Pie (make 1)

With size 3.00mm (UK 11, US 2) double-pointed needles and beige yarn, cast on 6 sts and divide between three needles; use fourth needle to knit.

Round 1: k.

Round 2: inc in each st [12 sts].

Round 3: (k1, inc 1) 6 times [18 sts].

Round 4: (k2, inc 1) 6 times [24 sts].

Round 5: (k3, inc 1) 6 times [30 sts].

Continue in this way, knitting 1 extra st between each increase, until there are 108 sts.

Next round: p to end.

Next round: (k1, p1) to end.

Rep last round twice more.

Next round: *k1, (p1, k1) 7 times, sl1, k2tog, psso, rep from * 5 times more [96 sts].

Next round: (k1, p1) to end.

Rep last round twice more.

Next round: *k1, (p1, k1) 6 times, sl1, k2tog, psso, rep from * 5 times more [84 sts].

Next round: (k1, p1) to end.

Next round: p.

Next round: (k5, k2tog) 12 times [72 sts].

Next round: (k10, k2tog) 6 times [66 sts].

Next round: (k9, k2tog) 6 times [60 sts].

Next round: (k8, k2tog) 6 times [54 sts].

Continue in this way, knitting 1 fewer st between each decrease, until there are 36 sts, then insert a circle of craft foam, approximately 9cm (3¾in) in diameter,

through the hole in the centre, to create a flat base.

Next round: (k4, k2tog) 6 times [30 sts].

Next round: (k3, k2tog) 6 times [24 sts].

Next round: (k2, k2tog) 6 times [18 sts].

Next round: (k1, k2tog] 6 times [12 sts].

Next round: (k2tog) 6 times [6 sts].

Cut yarn, leaving a tail, and thread through rem sts.

Crimped edge

Using size 3.00mm (UK 11, US 2) double-pointed needles, and distributing stitches between three needles, pick up and k 108 sts on purl ridge around top edge of pie.

Round 1: inc in each st [216 sts] and cast off.

Pastry leaves (make 3)

With size 3.00mm (UK 11, US 2) needles and beige yarn, cast on 1 st.

Row 1 (WS): inc 2 (k into front, back and front of st) [3 sts].

Row 2: k1, p1, k1.

Row 3: k1, inc 2 (as in row 1), k1 [5 sts].

Row 4: k1, (p1, k1) twice.

Row 5: k1, inc 1, p1, inc 1, k1 [7 sts].

Row 6: k1, (p2, k1) twice.

Row 7: k3, p1, k3.

Rows 8–11: Rep rows 6 and 7.

Row 12: Rep row 6.

Row 13: k1, k2tog, p1, k2tog, k1 [5 sts].

Row 14: k1, (p1, k1) twice.

Row 15: k1, sl1, k2tog, psso, k1 [3 sts].

Row 16: p3tog.

Fasten off.

Making up

Insert stuffing through the small hole in the centre of the pie, then pull up the tail of the yarn and fasten off. Stitch the pastry leaves to the top of the pie. The finished pie measures approximately 12cm (4¾in) in diameter.

Needles:

1 pair 3.00mm (UK 11; US 2) knitting needles

Set of four double-pointed 3.00mm (UK 11; US 2) knitting needles

Hearty Lunch

Creating a pie, with crisp pastry enclosing a delicious sweet or savoury filling, is a labour of love.

Prawn

Materials:

1 ball DK yarn – pink

Polyester fibrefill

Tapestry needle

Sewing needle and pink thread

Two small black beads for eyes

Needles:

1 pair 3.00mm (UK 11; US 2) knitting needles

Two 3.00mm (UK 11; US 2) double-pointed
   knitting needles

Instructions:

Head (make 1)

With size 3.00mm (UK 11; US 2) needles and
pink yarn, cast on 4 sts.
Row 1: k each st tbl.
Row 2: k to end.
Row 3: p to end.
Row 4: inc 1, p2, inc 1 [6 sts].
Row 5: k to end.
Row 6: inc 1, p to last st, inc 1.
Rep rows 5 and 6 twice more [12 sts].
Cast off.

Body (make 1)

With size 3.00mm (UK 11; US 2) needles and
pink yarn, cast on 10 sts.
Row 1: k to end.
Row 2: p to end.
Rows 3–4: g st.
Rows 5–12: rep rows 1–4 twice.
Rows 13: k2tog, k6, k2tog [8 sts].
Rows 14–17: Rep rows 1–4 once.
Row 18: p2tog, p4, p2tog [6 sts].
Rows 19–21: k to end.
Row 22: (p2tog) 3 times [3 sts].
Row 23: k to end.
Row 24: p to end.
Row 25: inc in each st [6 sts].
Row 26: inc in each st [12 sts].
Row 27: (k1, p1) to end.
Rep row 27 three times.
Cast off in rib and fasten off, leaving a tail of
yarn for sewing.

Antennae (make 1)

With size 3.00mm (UK 11; US 2) double-pointed
needles and pink yarn, cast on 2 sts.
Row 1: k2; do not turn but slide sts to other
end of needle.
Rep this row until work measures 10cm (4in);
fasten off.

Making up

Join the head to the body with the tapestry
needle and spare yarn. Run the tail of the
yarn down each edge of the body and pull
up slightly, to create a curved shape. Stitch
the edges of the body (not including the tail)
together and stuff lightly, then stuff the head
and close the seam. For legs, knot several
strands of yarn to the underside, at the base of
the head.

   Stitch two beads in place for eyes, one on
each side of the head, using a sewing needle
and pink thread, then fold the antennae piece
in half and stitch it to the head.

Prawn Again
*Prawns are a tasty seafood snack –
fresh, light and healthy!*

Sweetcorn

Materials:

1 ball DK cotton yarn – corn yellow
1 ball four-ply wool or acrylic yarn – light green
Polyester fibrefill (optional)
Tapestry needle

Needles:

1 pair of 2.75mm (UK 12; US 2) knitting needles
1 pair of 3.25mm (UK 10; US 3) knitting needles

Instructions:

Corn (make 1)

With 3.25mm (UK 10; US 3) needles and yellow yarn, cast on 28 sts.
Row 1: k.
Row 2: p.
Row 3: k1, (k2tog) 13 times, k1 [15 sts].
Row 4: k1, (M1, k1) 13 times, k1 [28 sts].
Rows 5–44: Rep rows 1–4.
Row 45: cast off 2, k to end [26 sts].
Row 46: cast off 2, k to end [24 sts].
Rows 47–97: Cont in garter stitch (k every row).
Cast off.

Leaf (make 3)

With 2.75mm (UK 12; US 2) needles and light green yarn, cast on 27 sts.
Row 1: k3, (sl1 purlwise with yarn at back of work, k3) 6 times.
Row 2: p.
Rows 3–32: Rep rows 1 and 2 15 times.
Row 33: k1, sl1, k1, psso, (sl1 purlwise, k1, sl1, k1, psso) 6 times.
Row 34: p.
Row 35: k2, (sl1 purlwise, k2) 6 times.
Row 36: p.
Rows 37–42: Rep rows 35 and 36.
Row 43: k2tog, (sl1 purlwise, k2tog) 6 times [13 sts].
Row 44: p.
Row 45: k1, (sl1 purlwise, k1) 6 times.
Row 46: p.
Rows 47–52: Rep rows 45 and 46.
Row 53: k1, (k2tog) 6 times [7 sts].
Row 54: p.
Row 55: k.
Row 56: p.
Rows 57–60: Rep rows 55 and 56.
Row 61: k1, (sl1, k2tog, psso) twice [3 sts].
Row 62: p; cut yarn and thread through rem sts.

Making up

Starting at the cast-off edge, roll up the corn to form a firm cob, adding stuffing where necessary. Slipstitch the cast-on row to hold it in place. Pull up the stitches at the base of each leaf and stitch each one to the base of the corn cob, overlapping them slightly. The finished corn cob measures approximately 15cm (5⅞in) long and 6.5cm (2½in) wide.

Knitting note

The instruction 'M1' requires you to make a stitch. To do this, pick up the strand in front of the next stitch to be worked, transfer it to the left-hand needle and knit into the back of the loop.

Corn on the Cob

Nestled in its protective leaves, the knobbly texture of the corn makes a fun and very recognisable novelty knit.

Apple

Materials:

2 balls DK wool or wool blend yarn – 1 green (A) and 1 red (B)

Small amount of DK yarn – brown

Polyester fibrefill

Tapestry needle

Needles:

1 pair 3.25mm (UK 10; US 3) knitting needles,

Two 3.00mm (UK 11; US 2) double-pointed knitting needles

Instructions:

Large green apple

With 3.25mm (UK 10; US 3) needles and green yarn, cast on 12 sts.
Row 1 (RS): k to end.
Row 2: p to end.
Row 3: inc1 in each st to end [24 sts].
Row 4: p to end.
Row 5: (inc1, k1) 12 times [36 sts].
Row 6: p to end.
Row 7: k1 (inc1, k2) 11 times, inc1, k1 [48 sts].
Rows 8–24: Beg with a p row, work in st st (1 row purl, 1 row knit).
Row 25: k1, k2tog, *k2, k2tog; rep from * to last st, k1 [36 sts].
Row 26: p to end.
Row 27: (k1, k2tog) 12 times [24 sts].
Row 28: (p2tog) 12 times [12 sts].
Row 29: (k2tog) 6 times [6 sts].
Cut yarn, leaving a tail. Thread through rem sts.

Small red and green apple

With two 3.00mm (UK 11; US 2) double-pointed needles and green yarn (A), cast on 12 sts.
Row 1 (RS): k to end.
Row 2: p to end.
Row 3: inc1 in each st to end [24 sts].
Row 4: p to end.
Row 5: (inc1, k1) 12 times [36 sts].
Continue in stocking stitch without further shaping, introducing red yarn (B) as follows:
Row 6: p13A, p12B, p12A.
Row 7: k11A, k14B, k11A.
Row 8: p10A, p16B, p10A.
Row 9: k9A, k18B, k9A.
Row 10: p8A, p20B, p8A.

Row 11: k7A, k22B, k7A.
Row 12: p6A, p24B, p6A.
Row 13: k5A, k26B, k5A.
Row 14: p4A, p28B, p4A.
Row 15: k3A, k30B, k3A.
Row 16: p2A, p32B, p2A. Cut green yarn (A) and continue with red (B).
Row 17: k to end.
Row 18: p to end.
Row 19: k to end.
Row 20: (p1, p2tog) 12 times [24 sts].
Row 21: (k2tog) 12 times [12 sts].
Row 22: (p2tog) 6 times [6 sts].
Cut yarn, leaving a tail. Thread through rem sts.

Stalk

With brown yarn and two 3.25mm double-pointed needles, cast on 3 sts.
Row 1: k3; do not turn but slide sts to other end of needle.
Rep row 1 until cord measures 4cm; cut yarn, leaving a tail, and fasten off.

Making up

Graft the sides (row ends) together to form a neat, invisible seam. Stuff the piece quite firmly with polyester fibrefill, then pull up the tail of the yarn to close the stitches on the last row. Close up the hole in the base in a similar way. Thread the tail of the yarn at the base of the stalk on to a tapestry needle and thread the needle down through the centre of the apple and pull slightly to create an indentation in the top. At the top of the stalk, thread the tail of the yarn in and out of the last two stitches to create a knobbly end. The finished apple measures approximately 6cm (2⅜in) high and 8cm (3⅛in) in diameter.

Scrumping!
Would you Adam 'n' Eve it? This pair of sweet-looking apples should be enough to tempt anyone.

Lemon Slice

Materials:

1 ball DK acrylic yarn – lemon yellow

Small amount DK acrylic yarn – white

Craft foam, 2mm (¹⁄₁₆in) thick

Tapestry needle and thread

Instructions:

Lemon slice

With set of five size 3.00mm (UK 11; US 2)
double-pointed needles and white yarn,
cast on 6 sts and distribute equally between
three needles.

Round 1: k all sts; cut white yarn and continue
in yellow.

Round 2: inc1 in each st [12 sts].

Round 3: (inc1, k1) 6 times [18 sts].

Round 4: (inc1, k2) 6 times [24 sts].

Round 5: (inc1, k3) 6 times [30 sts].

Round 6: (inc1, k4) 6 times [36 sts].

Round 7: (inc1, k5) 6 times [42 sts].

Round 8: (inc1, k6) 6 times [48 sts].

Join in white yarn (but do not cut yellow).

Round 9: with white yarn, (inc1, k7) 6 times
[54 sts].

With yellow yarn, knit 3 rounds.

Round 13: with white yarn, (k2tog, k7) 6 times
[48 sts].

Cut white yarn and continue in yellow.

Round 14: (k2tog, k6) 6 times [42 sts].

Round 15: (k2tog, k5) 6 times [36 sts].

Round 16: (k2tog, k4) 6 times [30 sts].

Round 17: (k2tog, k3) 6 times [24 sts].

Round 18: (k2tog, k2) 6 times [18 sts].

Round 19: (k2tog, k1) 6 times [12 sts].

Round 20: (k2tog) 6 times.

Cut yarn, leaving a tail, and thread
through
rem 6 sts.

Needles:

Set of five double-pointed 3.00mm (UK 11;
US 2) knitting needles

Making up

Cut a 6cm (2³⁄₈in) disc of 2mm (¹⁄₁₆in) craft
foam and insert it into the knitted shape.
Thread a tapestry needle with white yarn and
embroider lines radiating from the centre of
the lemon slice. Embroider pips in detached
chain stitch. The finished lemon slice measures
approximately 6cm (2³⁄₈in) in diameter.

Ice and a Slice

A slice of lemon is just the thing to add to a drink – a knitted drink, of course! If you prefer a lime slice, use green yarn and work as for lemon until round 6 has been completed. Change to white yarn and work round 7. Knit 3 rounds in green, then work round 13 in white and rounds 14 onwards in green. The finished lime slice is approximately 5.5cm (2¼in) in diameter.

Banana

Materials:

2 balls DK yarn – 1 yellow and 1 ivory

Polyester fibrefill

18cm (7in) zip – yellow

Sewing thread – yellow

Tapestry needle

Sewing needle

Needles:

1 pair 3.25mm (UK 10; US 3) knitting needles

1 set of four 2.75mm (UK 12; US 2) double-pointed knitting needles

Instructions:

Banana skin (make 1)

With size 3.25mm (UK 10; US 3) needles, cast on 12 sts in yellow yarn.

Row 1 (RS): (k2, p1) 4 times.

Row 2: (k1, p2) 4 times.

Rows 3–6: Rep rows 1 and 2 twice more.

Row 7: (inc 1, inc 1, p1) 4 times [20 sts].

Row 8: (k1, p4) 4 times.

Row 9: *(k1, inc 1) twice, p1, rep from * 3 times more [28 sts].

Row 10: (k1, p6) 4 times.

Row 11: (k6, p1) 4 times.

Rows 12–60: Rep rows 10 and 11, ending with row 10 to start the next knit row.

Row 61: (sl1, k1, psso, k2, k2tog, p1) 4 times [20 sts].

Row 62: (k1, p4) 4 times.

Row 63: (sl1, k1, psso, k2tog, p1) 4 times [12 sts].

Row 64: p2tog 6 times [6 sts].

Row 65: k.

Row 66: p.

Rows 67–70: Rep rows 65 and 66 twice more. Cast off knitwise; cut yarn, leaving a long tail for sewing up.

Banana (make 1)

With 2.75mm (UK 12; US 2) double-pointed knitting needles and ivory yarn, cast on 12 sts and divide between three needles.

Rounds 1 and 2: k.

Round 3: (k1, inc 1) 6 times [18 sts].

Round 4: k.

Round 5: (k2, inc 1) 6 times [24 sts].

Round 6: k.

Round 7: (k7, inc 1) 3 times [27 sts].

Rounds 8–64: k; or until work measures 18cm (7in) from beg.

Round 65: (k7, k2tog) 3 times [24 sts].

Round 66: k.

Round 67: (k2, k2tog) 6 times [18 sts].

Round 68: k.

Round 69: (k1, k2tog) 6 times [12 sts].

Round 70: k.

Break yarn and thread through rem sts.

Making up

Insert an 18cm (7in) zip in the banana skin. Stuff the banana and close the end by threading yarn through all the stitches. Pull up tightly and fasten off. The finished banana measures approximately 21cm (8¼in) long and 5cm (2in) in diameter.

Unzip a Banana
Instead of inserting a zip, graft the two long edges of the banana skin together and pull up the yarn tightly to shorten the seam, thereby causing the banana to bend. Before completing the seam, stuff the banana skin.

Fish 'n' Chips

Materials:

1 ball DK yarn – beige

1 ball wool/silk blend sock yarn – pale yellow

Polyester fibrefill

Craft foam, 1cm (⅜in) thick

Tapestry needle

Needles:

1 pair 2.25mm (UK 13; US 1) knitting needles

1 pair 2.75mm (UK 12; US 2) knitting needles

Instructions:

Fish in batter (make 2)

With size 2.75mm (UK 12; US 2) needles and beige yarn, cast on 5 sts.

Row 1: k1, (p1, k1) twice.

Row 2: as row 1.

Row 3: inc 1, p1, k1, p1, inc 1 [7 sts].

Row 4: p1, (k1, p1) three times.

Row 5: inc 1, k1, (p1, k1) twice, inc 1.

Row 6: k1, (p1, k1) to end.

Row 7: inc 1, p1, (k1, p1) three times, inc 1.

Row 8: p1, (k1, p1) to end.

Rows 9–12: rep rows 5–8 once more [15 sts].

Rows 13–14: p1, (k1, p1) to end.

Row 15: inc 1, k1, (p1, k1) six times, inc 1 [17 sts].

Row 16: k1, (p1, k1) to end.

Rows 17–26: rep row 16 11 times more.

Row 27: k1, k2tog, p1, (k1, p1) to last 3 sts, k2tog, k1 [15 sts].

Row 28: p1, (k1, p1) to end.

Rows 29–30: rep row 28.

Row 31: p1, p2tog, k1, (p1, k1) to last 3 sts, p2tog, p1 [13 sts].

Row 32: k1, (p1, k1) to end.

Rows 33–34: rep row 32.

Row 35: k1, k2tog, p1, (k1, p1) to last 3 sts, k2tog, k1 [11 sts].

Row 36: p1, (k1, p1) to end.

Row 37: p1, p2tog, k1, (p1, k1) to last 3 sts, p2tog, p1 [9 sts].

Row 38: k1, (p1, k1) to end.

Row 39: k1, k2tog, p1, k1, p1, k2tog, k1 [7 sts].

Rows 40–41: p1, (k1, p1) to end.

Row 42: inc 1, k1, (p1, k1) twice, inc 1 [9sts].

Row 43: k1, (p1, k1) to end.

Row 44: inc 1, p1, (k1, p1) three times, inc 1.

Row 45: p1, (k1, p1) to end.

Rows: 46–51: Rep row 45 six times more.

Cast off.

Chips (make at least 5)

With size 2.25mm (UK 13; US 1) needles and yellow yarn, cast on 17 sts.

Row 1: p to end.

Row 2 (RS): k to end.

Row 3: p to end.

Rows 4–5: as row 3.

Rows 6–14: rep rows 2–5 twice more.

Row 15: cast on 3 sts, k to end [20 sts].

Row 16: Cast on 3 sts, p to end [23 sts].

Cast off purlwise.

Chunky chips (make at least 5)

With size 2.25mm (UK 13; US 1) needles and yellow yarn, cast on 21 sts.

Row 1 (RS): k to end.

Row 2: p to end.

Row 3: k to end.

Row 4: p to end.

Rows 5–6: k to end.

Rows 7–18: rep rows 1–6 twice more.

Row 19: cast on 4 sts, k to end [25 sts].

Row 20: cast on 4 sts, p to end [29 sts].

Row 21: k to end.

Rows 22–23: p to end.

Cast off.

Making up

Stitch the two batter pieces together around the edges; leave a small gap and insert polyester fibrefill, then stitch the gap closed. Cut the foam into strips the same length as the chips. Place the foam on the WS of the work, adding a few wisps of polyester fibrefill for extra padding if necessary. Wrap the knitted fabric round and join the side and end seams using spare yarn. The finished fish measures approximately 14cm (5½in) long and 7cm (2¾in) wide, and the chips are approximately 7cm (2¾in) long. The chunky chips are a little larger at 8cm (3in) long.

Salt and Vinegar?

This classic British takeaway treat of fish in crisp batter, accompanied by golden chips, is irresistible. Garnish it with a sprig of parsley, following the instructions on page 24.

Noodles

Materials:

5 balls DK yarn – 1 beige, 1 white, 1 russet, 1 red and 1 green

1 ball 4-ply silk or rayon yarn – pale yellow

Tapestry needle

Needles:

1 pair 3.25mm (UK 10; US 3) knitting needles

Two double-pointed 3.00mm (UK 11; US 2) knitting needles

Instructions:

Noodles (make at least 20)
With size 3.00mm (UK 11; US 2) double-pointed needles and pale yellow yarn, cast on 3 sts.
Row 1: k3; do not turn but slide sts to other end of needle
Rep this row until cord measures approximately 30cm (12in) long.

Crispy pork slices (make at least 3)
With size 3.25mm needles and beige yarn, cast on 10 sts.
Break yarn and join in white.
Row 1: k each st tbl.
Row 2: sl1, k to end.
Row 3: rep row 2.
Break yarn and join in russet.
Row 4: k1, (k2tog, k) three times [7 sts].
Row 5: sl1, k to end.
Rows 6–14: rep row 5.
Cast off.

Spring onions and peppers (make 3 of each)
Using the same needles and exactly the same method as for the noodles, but knitting fewer rows, make short lengths of cord in green and white and red yarn to represent small pieces of the different vegetables.

Making up
Weave in all of the loose ends, then arrange the noodles in a cardboard Chinese food carton and scatter the other items on top.

Pork Chow Mein!
Eaten straight from the takeaway carton, noodles are a satisfying snack, especially with a few tasty slices of crispy pork alongside delicious shreds of spring onion and red pepper.

Shish Kebab

Materials:

3 balls wool or acrylic DK yarn – 1 brown,
   1 green and 1 red

1 ball of cotton DK yarn – beige

Craft foam, or washing-up sponge 2.5cm
   (1in) thick

Polyester fibrefill

Wooden or bamboo skewers

Tapestry needle

Instructions:

Meat cube (make 3)

With size 3.25mm (UK 10; US 3) needles and
brown DK yarn, cast on 6 sts.
Rows 1–9: p.
Rows 10–18: k.
Rows 19–27: p.
Row 28: cast on 7 sts, k6, p1, k6 [13 sts].
Row 29: cast on 7 sts, k6, p1, k6, p1, k6 [20 sts].
Rep last row 8 times more. Cast off.

Pepper chunk (make 3 in red and 2 in green)

With 3.25mm (UK 10; US 3) needles and red or
green DK yarn, cast on 21 sts.
Row 1: k10 tbl, p1, k10 tbl.
Row 2: k10, p1, k10.
Rows 3–4: rep row 2.
Row 5: k1, (k2tog, k1) 3 times, p1, (k1, k2tog) 3
times, k1 [15 sts].
Row 6: k7, p1, k7.
Rows 7–9: rep row 6.
Row 10: k1, (k2tog, k1) twice, p1, (k1, k2tog)
twice, k1 [11 sts].
Row 11: k5, p1, k5.
Rows 12–14: rep row 11.
Cast off, leaving a tail of yarn for sewing up.

Mushroom (make 3)

With four 3.00mm (UK 11; US 2) double-
pointed needles and beige DK yarn, cast on 6
sts and divide between three needles.
Round 1: k to end.
Round 2: inc in each st [12 sts].
Round 3: k to end.
Round 4: (k1, inc 1) 6 times [18 sts].
Round 5: k to end.

Needles:

1 pair 3.25mm (UK 10; US 3) knitting needles

Set of four double-pointed 3.00mm (UK 11;
US 2) knitting needles

Round 6: (k2, inc 1) 6 times [24 sts].
Round 7: k to end.
Round 8: (k3, inc 1) 6 times [30 sts].
Rounds 9 and 10: k to end.
Round 11: (k3, k2tog tbl) 6 times [24 sts].
Round 12: (k2, k2tog tbl) 6 times [18 sts].
Round 13: (k1, k2tog tbl) 6 times [12 sts].
Round 14: (k2tog) 6 times [6 sts].
Rounds 15–20: k.
Break yarn and thread through rem sts.

Making up

Cut a cube of craft foam or washing-up sponge
to fit inside the cube of meat. Place it on
the wrong side of the work and draw up the
knitted fabric to enclose it. Stitch the seams by
oversewing edges with the tapestry needle and
spare yarn. For the pepper, fold the work in half
and oversew the edges. Stuff the mushroom
firmly and tie off the end of the stalk. Push
a wooden or bamboo skewer through the
knitted pieces, in any order you like. The meat
cubes are approximately 3.5cm (1¼in) and the
mushrooms are 4cm (1½in) in diameter.

Any Sauce With That?
*Comprising chunks of meat, skewered and grilled,
sometimes with vegetables, the shish kebab is one of the
tastiest treats to come from the Middle East and is easy
to replicate using yarn and needles. Make a vegetarian
version, if you like, with mushrooms replacing the meat.*

Materials:

1 ball DK yarn – beige

1 ball aran weight wool yarn – deep pink

Craft foam, 2.5cm (1in) thick

Polyester fibrefill

Tapestry needle

Needles:

1 pair 3.25mm (UK 10; US 3) knitting needles

1 pair 3.75mm (UK 9; US 5) knitting needles

Instructions:

Pastry (made in 1 piece):

With size 3.25mm (UK 10; US 3) needles
and beige yarn, cast on 24 sts.

Row 1: p to end.

Row 2: k to end.

Row 3: p to end.

Row 4: k1, (yfwd, k2tog) to last st, k1.

Row 5: p to end.

Row 6: k to end.

Row 7: To form crimped edge of pastry,
fold work and k each st together with
corresponding st from cast-on row.

Outer edge

Starting with a k row, continue in stocking stitch
for 10 rows.

Purl 2 rows.

Base

Next row: k1, sl1, k1, psso, k to last 3 sts,
k2tog, k1.

Next row: p to end.

Next row: k to end.

Next row: p to end.

Rep last 4 rows until 6 sts rem.

Next row: k1, sl1, k1, psso, k2tog, k1.

Next row: p to end.

Next row: k to end.

Next row: p to end.

Next row: (k2tog) twice.

Next row: p2tog.

Fasten off.

Top crust

With WS facing, pick up and k 24 sts along
lower edge of hem on crimped edge. Work as
for base.

Cherry filling (make 1)

With size 3.75mm (UK 9; US 5) needles, cast on
47 sts.

Row 1: k2, then k1, yfwd, k1, yfwd, k1 into
same stitch; turn and p5; turn and k5; turn, sl2
knitwise, k3tog, psso. Repeat another fourteen
times, k2.

Row 2: p to end.

Row 3: k4, then k1, yfwd, k1, yfwd, k1 into
same stitch; turn and p5; turn and k5; turn, sl2
knitwise, k3tog, psso. Repeat 14 times, k1.

Row 4: p to end.

Cast off.

Making up

Cut a wedge of foam to fill the pastry. Pad
out with a few wisps of polyester fibrefill all
round. Stitch the edges of the filling to the top
and base of pastry. The finished slice of pie
measures 15cm (6in) long, 10cm (4in) wide and
4cm (1½in) deep.

Sweet Ol' Blueberry Pie

A slice of pie is a wonderful indulgence… especially when it has a juicy, fruity filling as shown here. For the blueberry filling, which does not involve knitting bobbles, use a purple bouclé yarn. With 3.25mm (UK 10; US 3) needles, cast on 8 sts and work in garter stitch (knit every row) to make a strip 25cm (10in) long.

Iced Doughnut

Materials:

1 ball acrylic blend DK yarn – white with coloured flecks

1 ball acrylic or wool yarn – light beige

Polyester fibrefill

Tapestry needle

Needles:

Set of four 3.00mm (UK 11; US 2) double-pointed knitting needles

Instructions:

Doughnut

With size 3.00mm (UK 11; US 2) double-pointed needles and white yarn with coloured flecks, cast on 60 sts and divide between three needles.

Rounds 1–5: k to end.

Round 6: (k4, k2tog) 10 times [50 sts].

Rounds 7–8: knit 2 rounds.

Round 9: (k3, k2tog) 10 times [40 sts].

Rounds 10–11: knit 2 rounds.

Round 12: (k2, k2tog) 10 times [30 sts].

Rounds 13–14: knit 2 rounds.

Round 15: (k1, k2tog) 10 times [20 sts].

Rounds 16–17: knit 2 rounds. Break yarn; join in light beige.

Rounds 18–19: knit 2 rounds.

Round 20: (k1, inc 1) 10 times [30 sts].

Rounds 21–22: knit 2 rounds.

Round 23: (k2, inc 1) 10 times [40 sts].

Rounds 24–25: knit 2 rounds.

Round 26: (k3, inc 1) 10 times [50 sts].

Rounds 27–28: knit 2 rounds.

Round 29: (k4, inc 1) 10 times [60 sts].

Rounds 30–31: knit 2 rounds.

Cast off, leaving a tail of yarn for sewing up.

Making up

Thread the tapestry needle with the tail of yarn and, with the right side facing outwards, stitch the cast-on and cast-off edges together, leaving a small gap. Stuff the doughnut with polyester fibrefill until it is firm, then sew the gap closed. The finished doughnut measures approximately 10cm (4in) in diameter and is 3.5cm (1⅜in) thick.

Raspberry Doughnut

Definitely not a health food! Doughnuts are a very popular sweet snack, and come in a myriad of flavours. Instead of a speckled yarn, use a soft angora or mohair blend in deep raspberry pink and use a sewing needle and thread to stitch on clear glass seed beads in a random pattern to represent a light dusting of sugar crystals.

Ice Cream

Materials:

1 ball cotton 4-ply yarn – straw yellow

1 ball soft bouclé yarn – white

1 ball acrylic DK yarn – chocolate brown

Craft foam, 2mm (1/16in) thick

Polyester fibrefill

Tapestry needle

Needles:

Set of four 2.75mm (UK 12; US 2) double-
pointed knitting needles

1 pair 4.00mm (UK 8; US 6) knitting needles

Instructions:

Cone (make 2)

With set of four 2.75mm (UK 12; US 2) needles
and straw yellow yarn, cast on 6 sts and divide
between three needles.

Round 1: (k1, p1) 3 times.

Round 2: as round 1.

Round 3: k to end.

Rounds 4–5: as round 1.

Round 6: inc in each st to end [12 sts].

Rounds 7–8: (k1, p1) 6 times.

Round 9: k to end.

Rounds 10–11: (k1, p1) 6 times.

Round 12: (inc 1, k2, inc 1) 3 times [18 sts].

Rounds 13–14: (k1, p1) 9 times.

Round 15: k to end.

Rounds 16–17: (k1, p1) 9 times.

Round 18: (inc 1, k4, inc 1) 3 times [24 sts].

Rounds 19–20: (k1, p1) 12 times.

Round 21: k to end.

Rounds 22–23: (k1, p1) 12
times.

Round 24: (inc 1, k3) 6
times [30 sts].

Rounds 25–26: (k1, p1)
15 times.

Round 27: k to end.

Rounds 28–29: (k1, p1)
15 times.

Round 30: (inc 1, k4) 6 times [36 sts].

Rounds 31–32: (k1, p1) 18 times.

Round 33: k to end.

Rounds 34–35: (k1, p1) 18 times.

Round 36: (inc 1, k5) 6 times [42 sts].

Rounds 37–38: (k1, p1) 21 times.

Round 39: k to end.

Rounds 40–41: (k1, p1) 21 times.

Round 42: (inc 1, k6) 6 times [48 sts].

Rounds 43–44: (k1, p1) 24 times.

Round 45: k to end.

Rounds 46–47: (k1, p1) 24 times.

Round 48: (p1, k1) to end.

Round 49: (k1, p1) to end.

Rounds 50–53: rep rounds 48 and 49 twice.

Cast off.

Soft scoop (make 1)

With size 4.00mm (UK 8; US 6) needles and
white yarn, cast on 24 sts.

Rows 1–2: st st. Begin with a k row.

Row 3: (k3, inc 1) to end [30 sts].

Rows 4–6: st st. Begin with a p row.

Row 7: (k4, inc 1) to end [36 sts].

Rows 8–10: st st. Begin with a p row.

Row 11: (k5, inc 1) to end [42 sts].

Rows 12–14: st st. Begin with a p row.

Row 15: (k6, inc 1) to end [48 sts].

Row 16: p to end.

Row 17: (k6, k2tog) to end [42 sts].

Row 18: p to end.

Row 19: (k5, k2tog) to end [36 sts].

Rows 20–24: st st. Begin with a p row.

Row 25: (k4, k2tog) to end [30 sts].

Row 26: p to end.

Row 27: (k3, k2tog) to end [24 sts].

Row 28: p to end.

Row 29: (k2, k2tog) to end [18 sts].

Row 30: p to end.

Row 31: (k1, k2tog) to end [12 sts].

Row 32: p to end.

Row 33: (k2tog) 6 times [6 sts].

Rows 34–38: st st. Begin with a p row.

Row 39: (k2tog) 3 times [3 sts].

Row 40: p3.

Row 41: sl1, k2tog, psso; fasten off, leaving a
tail of yarn for sewing.

Chocolate flake (make 1)

With 4.00mm (UK 8; US 6) needles and brown DK yarn, cast on 20 sts.

Row 1: (k1, p1) to end.

Rep row 1 until work measures 10cm (4in). Cast off ribwise.

Making up

Cut a semicircle of craft foam, roll it into a cone and place it inside the knitted cone, making sure that the edges are below the cast-off edge. Stuff the cone with polyester fibrefill. Roll up the flake and secure it by stitching with the tapestry needle and spare yarn. Create small pleats in the fabric of the soft scoop and secure it with a few firm stitches, then stitch up the seam, leaving a gap about halfway down. Insert the chocolate flake into the gap, then stuff firmly. Stitch the soft scoop to the cone on the inside of the rim. The finished ice cream measures approximately 22cm (8¾in) tall.

Round scoop for the strawberry ice cream (make 1)

With set of four 2.75mm (UK 12; US 2) needles and pink yarn, cast on 24 sts and divide between three needles.

Round 1: k to end.

Round 2: p to end.

Round 3: (k3, inc 1) 6 times [30 sts].

Rounds 4–5: k.

Round 6: (k4, inc 1) 6 times [36 sts].

Rounds 7–8: k.

Round 9: (k5, inc 1) 6 times [42 sts].

Rounds 10–11: k.

Round 12: (k6, inc 1) 6 times [48 sts].

Strawberry Dream

A scoop of delicious ice cream in a crisp, biscuity cone is a great reminder of sunshine and days out. Making the round scoop with pink yarn will produce a mouth-watering strawberry cornet.

Rounds 13–16: k to end.

Round 17: (k6, k2tog) 6 times [42 sts].

Round 18: k to end.

Round 19: (k5, k2tog) 6 times [36 sts].

Cont in this way, working 1 fewer st between decreases on every other round, until 12 sts rem.

Next round: (k2tog) 6 times [6 sts].

Break yarn and thread through rem sts. Pull up and fasten off.

Ice Lolly

Materials:

4 skeins tapestry yarn – 1 bright pink, 1 yellow,
 1 green and 1 light brown

Craft foam, 2mm (¹⁄₁₆in) thick

Polyester fibrefill

Tapestry needle and thread

Flat wooden lolly stick

Needles:

2 pairs 3.00mm (UK 11; US 2) knitting needles

Instructions:

Lolly (make 2)
*With size 3.00mm (UK 11; US 2) needles
and pink yarn, cast on 7 sts.
Row 1: k each st tbl.
Row 2: p to end.**
Break yarn and transfer work to a spare
needle.
Rep from * to **.
Row 3: k to end, cast on 2 sts, k across sts on
spare needle [16 sts].
Row 4: p to end.
Rows 5–16: st st. Begin with a k row. Break yarn;
join in yellow.
Rows 17–28: st st. Begin with a k row. Break
yarn; join in green.
Rows 29–34: st st. Begin with a k row.
Row 35: k1, sl1, k1, psso, k to last 3 sts,
k2tog, k1 [14 sts].
Row 36: p to end.
Rows 37–40: Rep rows 35 and 36 twice more
[6 sts].
Cast off.

Stick (make 1)
*With size 3.00mm (UK 11; US 2) needles and
light brown yarn, cast on 7 sts.
Beg with a k row, work 20 rows in st st. Break
yarn, leaving a 25cm (10in) tail; thread through
all sts.

Making up
Pull up the tail of the yarn at the base of the
stick, then stitch the sides together. Insert the
lolly stick. Cut a piece of foam to fit inside the
lolly; pad out on both sides with polyester
fibrefill. Stitch the side seams of the lolly
using the tapestry needle and spare yarn to
match. Insert the end of the stick into the
base of the lolly and stitch the cast-on edges
together, securing the lolly to the stick with a
few neat stitches. The finished lolly measures
approximately 19cm (7½in) long (including
stick) and 6cm (2⅜in) wide.

Yarn note
You could use any DK weight yarn for this
project; as so little of each colour is needed,
small skeins of tapestry wool, available in a
dazzling choice of colours, are an ideal choice.

Popsicle

Straight from the freezer, what could be more refreshing on a hot day? For a woolly version of this frozen delight, use the most colourful yarns in your basket. Use your own combination of colours, such as three different shades of orange, to suggest juicy fruit flavours. If the lolly is designed as play food for a child, do not use a wooden stick.

Cherry Cupcake

Materials:

4 balls DK yarn – 1 white, 1 beige, 1 pink and 1 red

Craft foam, 2mm (¹⁄₁₆in) thick

Polyester fibrefill

Tapestry needle

Needles:

Set of four 3.00mm (UK 11; US 2) double-pointed knitting needles

1 pair 3.75mm (UK 9; US 5) knitting needles

1 pair 3.00mm (UK 11; US 2) knitting needles

Instructions:

Cake case (make 1)

With the set of four size 3.00mm (UK 11; US 2) double-pointed needles and white yarn, cast on 6 sts and distribute them between three needles.

Round 1: k to end.
Round 2: inc in each st [12 sts].
Round 3: (k1, inc 1) 6 times [18 sts].
Round 4: (k2, inc 1) 6 times [24 sts].
Round 5: (k3, inc 1) 6 times [30 sts].
Round 6: (k4, inc 1) 6 times [36 sts].
Round 7: (k5, inc 1) 6 times [42 sts].
Round 8: (k1, p1) to end.
Rounds 9–19: Rep round 8.
Round 20: (yfwd, k2tog) to end.
Rounds 21–25: Rep round 8.
Cast off, leaving a tail of yarn for sewing.

Cake (make 1)

With 3.00mm (UK 11; US 2) needles and beige yarn, cast on 6 sts.
Work in g st until work measures 18cm (7in). Cast off.

Icing (make 1)

With 3.75mm (UK 9; US 5) needles and pink yarn, cast on 9 sts.
Row 1: k to end.
Row 2: p to end.
Rep rows 1 and 2 until work measures 40cm (15¾in). Cast off.

Cherry (make 1)

With 3.00mm (UK 11; US 2) needles and red yarn, cast on 3 sts.
Row 1: inc 1, k to last st, inc 1.
Row 2: p to end.
Rows 3–6: Rep rows 1 and 2 twice [9 sts].
Row 7: k to end.

Row 8: p to end.
Row 9: k2tog, k to last 2 sts, k2tog.
Rows 10–13: Rep rows 8 and 9 twice [3 sts].
Cast off, leaving a tail of yarn.

Making up

Fold the last five rows of the cake case to the inside and slip stitch into place. To make the cake, join the ends of the beige piece to make a ring; insert this into the case and slip stitch it in place. At this stage, if you wish, cut a circle of craft foam to place in the bottom of the cake case, to create a stable, flat base. Fold the icing in half lengthways and stitch the sides together using the tapestry needle and thread. Roll up the folded icing into a spiral, securing it with a few stitches, then insert it into the centre of the case. To make the cherry, thread the tapestry needle with the tail of yarn and run the needle in and out of stitches all round the edge of the knitted piece. Place a ball of stuffing in the centre and pull up tightly, enclosing the filling, to create a ball shape. Stitch it to the top of the cake. The finished cake is approximately 5cm (2in) high and 7.5cm (3in) in diameter.

Lemon Fancy

This dainty teatime treat could easily be gobbled up in a couple of mouthfuls. A luxury yarn has been used to make the icing on these cakes but you could use any double-knitting weight yarn you like. If the cake is to be used as a decoration (and not as play food for children) you could decorate the top with a little flower, using 40cm (15¾in) of narrow purple ribbon for the petals and 9cm (3½in) of wire-edged green ribbon to make leaves.

Samosa

Materials:

1 ball cotton DK yarn – yellow ochre

Polyester fibrefill

Tapestry needle and thread

Needles:

1 pair 3.25mm (UK 10; US 3) knitting needles

Instructions:

Samosa

With size 3.25mm (UK 10; US 3) needles
and yellow ochre yarn, cast on 49 sts.
Row 1: sl1, k to end.
Row 2: k1, k2tog, k to last 3 sts, k2tog, k1.
Row 3: sl1, k to end.
Row 4: rep row 3.
Rep rows 2–4 until 5 sts remain.
Next row: k1, sl1, k2tog, psso, k1 [3 sts].
Next row: k to end.
Next row: sl1, k2tog, psso; fasten off.

Making up

Fold, bringing the point at the top of the triangle (where
the work was fastened off) to the centre of the cast-on
row, then fold in the two sides, forming a triangle of four
layers. Stitch the edges together, adding a little stuffing
for a plump result.

Fusion Food

*The samosa is a crispy Indian snack comprising a spicy
filling encased in a tempting triangle of pastry, and it is
a firm favourite the world over.
Spring rolls and samosas are from different culinary
traditions but these knitted versions pair up very nicely.
The finished samosa, knitted in a cotton yarn, with
an exotic saffron hue, measures approximately 10cm
(4in) long. To make the spring roll, use a wool DK yarn
in medium-brown and, instead of folding the knitted
fabric into a triangle, roll it up, tucking in the sides as
you go, then secure with a few stitches.*

Biscuit

Materials:

1 ball DK yarn – biscuit beige

1 ball soft bouclé yarn – white

Craft foam, 2mm (¹⁄₁₆in) thick

Tapestry needle

Needles:

1 set of four 3.00mm (UK 11; US 2) double-pointed knitting needles

1 set of four 4.00mm (UK 8; US 6) double-pointed knitting needles

Instructions:

Basic biscuit (make 2)

With set of four size 3.00mm (UK 11; US 2) needles and biscuit beige yarn, cast on 6 sts and divide equally between three needles.
Round 1: k to end.
Round 2: inc in each st to end [12 sts].
Round 3: (k1, inc 1) 6 times [18 sts].
Round 4: (k2, inc 1) 6 times [24 sts].
Round 5: (k3, inc 1) 6 times [30 sts].
Round 6: (k4, inc 1) 6 times [36 sts].
Round 7: (k5, inc 1) 6 times [42 sts].
Round 8: (k6, inc 1) 6 times [48 sts].
Round 9: (k7, inc 1) 6 times [54 sts].
Round 10: (k8, inc 1) 6 times [60 sts].
Round 11: k to end.
Round 12: (k8, k2tog) 6 times [54 sts].
Round 13: (k7, k2tog) 6 times [48 sts].
Round 14: (k6, k2tog) 6 times [42 sts].
Do not cast off but break yarn, leaving a long tail. Thread this through rem sts.

Creamy filling (make 1)

With set of four size 4.00mm (UK 8; US 6) needles and white yarn, cast on 6 sts and divide equally between three needles.
Rounds 1–8: Follow the instructions for the basic biscuit.
Round 9: k to end.
Round 10: (k6, k2tog) 6 times [42 sts].
Round 11: (k5, k2tog) 6 times [36 sts].
Do not cast off but break yarn, leaving a long tail. Thread this through rem sts.

Making up

Cut a circle of foam 6cm (2¼in) in diameter and place it on the wrong side of the knitted biscuit. Pull up the yarn until the knitting fits snugly, then fasten it off. Do the same with the creamy filling but use a 5.5cm (2⅛in) circle of foam.

To make a custard cream, sandwich the filling between two biscuits.

Knitting notes

The finished biscuit measures approximately 6.5cm (2½in) in diameter and 1.5–2cm (½–¾in) thick.

Milk and Cookies

Most people like a biscuit to accompany a cup of tea or coffee and fill the gap between meals, and they make a lovely pre-bedtime treat. Here are knitted versions of a couple of old favourites.
To make a chocolate biscuit, use chocolate brown double-knitting yarn and follow the instructions for the basic biscuit, omitting rounds 10 and 12. Stitch this topping to a single basic biscuit, with right sides up.

Chocolate Gateau

Materials:

2 balls double knitting – 1 chocolate and 1 cream

1 ball fluffy polyester yarn – cream

18 small, brown wooden beads

Cardboard for insert, 9 x 37cm (3½ x 14½in)

Toy stuffing

Needles:

1 pair 3.25mm (UK 10; US 3) knitting needles

Instructions:

Back and top of gateau

Cast on 14 sts in chocolate.
Rows 1–10: st st, starting with a K row.
Rows 11–14: change to fluffy yarn. Continue in st st.
Rows 15–24: change back to chocolate and continue in st st.
Row 25: purl across a knit row.
Rows 26–30: ** starting with a P row, work in st st.
Row 31: K1, K2tog, K to last 3 sts, K2tog, K1.
Rows 32–34: starting with a P row, work in st st.
Row 35: K1, K2tog to last 3 sts, K2tog, K1.
Rows 36–38: starting with a P row, work in st st.
Row 39: K1, K2tog, knit to last 3 sts, K2tog, K1.

Rows 40–42: starting with a P row, work in st st.
Row 43: K1, K2tog, K2, K2tog, K1.
Rows 44–46: starting with a P row, work in st st.
Row 47: K1, K2tog, K2tog, K1.
Row 48: purl.
Row 49: K2tog, K2tog.
Row 50: purl.
Row 51: K2tog. Break yarn and pull thread through last stitch. **

Base of gateau

Pick up and knit 14 sts across the cast-on row of the gateau back. Starting with a purl row work exactly as the top of the gateau from ** to **.

Sides of gateau

The sides of the gateau are knitted in one piece.

Cast on 48 sts in chocolate.
Rows 1–10: st st.
Rows 11–14: change to fluffy yarn. Continue in st st.
Rows 15–24: change back to chocolate and continue in st st.
Cast off.

Piped cream

Make two lengths of 3 chocolate cream swirls; two lengths with 3 light-coloured cream swirls; one length with 2 light-coloured cream swirls; and a single light-coloured cream swirl.

Cast on 1 st in chocolate or cream.
Row 1: ** K1, P1, K1, P1, K1 into the cast-on stitch [5 sts].
Row 2: slip 1, K3, leave the last st unworked. Work on the 3 centre sts until row 6.
Row 3: P3, leave last st.
Row 4: K3, leave last st.
Row 5: P3, leave last st.
Row 6: K4.
Row 7: P1, P2tog, P2tog.
Row 8: K2tog, K1.
Row 9: P2tog. ** [1 st].
Break yarn and pull through the remaining stitch – this will make a single cream swirl. To make a length of piped cream, repeat rows 1–9 from ** to **.

Making up

Attach one short edge of the gateau side to the back edge of the cake, making sure that the strips of cream-coloured gateau filling line up correctly. Repeat for the other side. Sew on the gateau base. Fold the strip of cardboard into a triangular shape and fit it inside the gateau to line the sides and back of the cake. It is important to make the cardboard shape slightly larger than the knitting, so that the knitting is stretched as it is sewn in place. This will make a neater finish. Stuff the cake with toy stuffing and sew on the top. Sew the two lengths of chocolate cream swirls to the back of the gateau – one along the bottom edge and one along the top edge. Attach the light-coloured cream swirls to the top of the gateau, then sew on the wooden beads.

Coffee Cupcake

Materials:

2 balls pure merino – 1 cream and 1 coffee

1 ball 100% cotton 4 ply – white

Pearl bead

60mm (2¼in) polystyrene craft ball

Toy stuffing

Instructions:

Top of cake

Cast on 40 sts in cream wool using
4mm needles.

Rows 1–4: st st for 4 rows.

Rows 5–10: change to coffee and g st for
6 rows.

Row 11: (k4, k2tog) to last 4 sts, k4 [34 sts].

Row 12: knit.

Row 13: knit, decreasing 6 sts randomly across
row [28 sts].

Row 14: knit.

Row 15: knit, decreasing 4 sts randomly across
row [24 sts].

Row 16: knit.

Break yarn, leaving a long end. Thread through
stitches on needle and draw up tightly.

Side of case

Cast on 60 sts using white cotton 4 ply and
2.25mm needles.

Rows 1–11: k1, p1 across row for 11 rows.

Row 12: inc every second p st across row.
Cast off.

Base of case

Cast on 10 sts using white cotton 4 ply and
2.25mm needles. Work in st st.

Row 1: * purl.

Row 2: knit, increasing 1 st at beg and end
of row. *

Rows 3–8: repeat rows 1 and 2 from * to *
[18 sts].

Rows 9–11: continue in st st.

Rows 12–18: dec 1 st at beg and end of every k
row [10 sts].

Row 19: purl.

Cast off.

Needles:

1 pair 4mm (UK 8; US 6) knitting needles

1 pair 2.25mm (UK 13; US 1) knitting needles

1 pair 3.25mm (UK 10; US 3) knitting needles

Opposite:

*The mocha cupcake is stitched in chocolate-
coloured wool and decorated with dark
wooden beads.*

Flower

Using 3.25mm needles and cream follow the
instruction for a single swirl of piped cream on
page 58. Break yarn and thread it through the
single stitch on the needle. Repeat for
each petal.

Making up

Join the side seam of the cupcake case, then
stitch the bottom in place. Join the side
seam of the cupcake top. Pull up the thread
holding the stitches at the top of the cake,
and darn the thread end in to hold it firmly in
place. Attach the petals to the top of the cake,
adding a bead to the centre. Using cream wool,
make French knots on the top of the cake.
Position the cake top inside the cupcake case.
Insert a polystyrene craft ball, adding some
stuffing to pad out the shape, then catch stitch
the top to the bottom.

Birthday Cake

Materials:

2 balls double knitting – 1 pink and 1 cream

Small amount pure merino – cream

Small amount double knitting – dark pink

2 red bugle beads

4 pink seed beads

12mm (½in) pink ribbon, 80cm (31½in)

Cardboard for insert, 10 x 51cm (4 x 20in)

Drinking straw

Needles:

1 pair 3.25mm (UK 10; US 3) knitting needles

Instructions:

Top and base of cake

For cake top, cast on 25 sts in pink.

Rows 1–25: st st.

Cast off. Repeat for the base.

Sides of cake

The sides of the cake are knitted in one piece.

Cast on 78 sts in pink.

Rows 1–28: st st.

Cast off.

Flower

Cast on 28 sts in pink.

Row 1: (k1, cast off 5 sts) to end [8 sts].

Break yarn and use a needle to pull it through the remaining 8 sts – this will make four petals. Secure the wool end with a few stitches to hold the petals together.

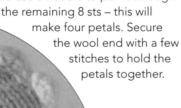

Candle

Cast on 17 sts using cream pure merino.

Rows 1–5: st st.

Cast off.

Flame

Cast on 2 sts in dark pink.

Row 1: knit.

Row 2: inc every st [4 sts].

Rows 3–4: knit.

Row 5: repeat row 2 [6 sts].

Rows 6–7: knit.

Row 8: k2tog, k2, k2tog [4 sts].

Rows 9–10: knit.

Row 11: k2tog, k2tog [2 sts].

Row 12: k2tog.

Piped cream

Make two lengths of piped cream in cream double knitting, each with 16 cream swirls, following the instructions on page 58.

Making up

From the cardboard make a box 10cm (4in) long x 7.5cm (3in) wide x 9.5cm (3¾in) deep. Make a small hole in the centre top for the candle. Wrap the knitted side panel around the box with the seam at the centre back. Sew the edges together with matching wool. Place the top and base of the cake in place and stitch to the edges of the side panel. Stitch the piped cream swirls around the top and bottom edges of the cake. Using cream wool, make French knots in a pattern on the sides and top of the cake. Stitch the pink flower to the to p of the cake, directly over the hole in the cardboard. For the candle, wrap the rectangle of knitting around the drinking straw and stitch it in place – the straw should be left longer than the stitching so that it can be pushed down into the box. Push the drinking straw into the hole in the box through the knitting. Secure with a few neat stitches. Stitch seed beads to each flower petal. Attach the flame to the candle, adding a bugle bead to each side. Tie the pink ribbon around the cake.

Fruit Tart

Materials:

1 ball 4 ply – beige

1 ball fluffy mohair acrylic mix – cream

Small amounts of 4 ply in pink, orange and yellow

Small amounts of double knitting in red and mauve

Small amounts of cotton yarn in lime green

Black, red and pink seed beads

Jar lid for pastry case insert, approximately 8cm (3¼in) diameter

Toy stuffing

Needles:

1 pair 3.25mm (UK 10; US 3) knitting needles

Set of four 2.25mm (UK 13; US 1) double-pointed knitting needles

Instructions:

Tart case

Using 4 ply beige, cast on 96 sts with double-ended needles – 32 sts on each of 3 needles.
Rounds 1–11: (k2, p2) for 11 rounds.
Round 12: purl.
Round 13: knit, decreasing 2 sts randomly on each needle.
Continue decreasing on each round until 1 st remains on each needle. Break yarn and pull through the remaining 3 sts.

Cream for inside tart

Using 3.25mm needles and cream, cast on 10 sts.
Rows 1–2: st st, starting with a k row.
Row 3: (k1, inc 1 st) 5 times across row [15 sts].
Row 4: purl.
Row 5: (k1, inc 1 st) to end [22 sts].
Row 6: purl.
Row 7: (k1, inc 1 st) to end [33 sts].
Row 8: purl.
Row 9: (k1, inc 1 st) to end [49 sts].
Rows 10–24: continue in st st.
Row 25: (k2tog, k1) to end [33 sts].

Row 26: purl.
Row 27: (k2tog, k1) to end [22 sts].
Row 28: purl.
Row 29: (k2tog, k1) to end [15 sts].
Row 30: purl.
Row 31: (k2tog, k1) to end [10 sts].
Row 32: purl.
Cast off.

Orange and lemon slices and raspberries

Make one orange slice, one lemon slice and three raspberries.

Using 3.25mm needles and appropriate colour, cast on 2 sts. Work in st st, starting with a k row.
Row 1: ** * inc every st to end [4 sts].
Row 2: purl.
Row 3: inc every st to end [8 sts].
Row 4: purl. *
Row 5: inc every st to end [16 sts].
Row 6: purl. **
Cast off.

Berries and kiwi slices

Make eleven berries and two kiwi slices.

Using 3.25mm needles and mauve or lime green, cast on 2 sts and work as given for slices and raspberries from * to *.
Row 5: k2tog to end [4sts].
Row 6: purl.
Row 7: k2tog to end [2sts].
Row 8: p2tog.
Break yarn and thread it through the last stitch.

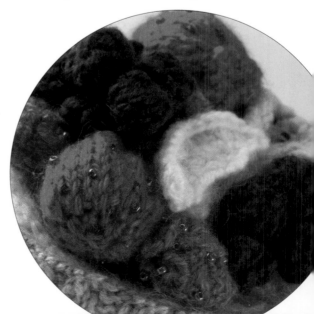

Strawberries

Make two strawberries.

Cast on 2 sts using 3.25mm needles and red wool.
Work 2 rows in st st.
Work as for slices and raspberries from ** to **.
Next row: inc every st to end [32 sts].
Starting with a p row, work in st st for 7 rows.
Cast off.

Making up

To finish each kiwi slice, stitch black seed beads in a circle on both sides. Sew up the side seam of each raspberry with right sides together – you will have a funnel shape. Turn right-side out. Insert a small ball of toy stuffing, pushing it well down into the raspberry.

Use the same coloured wool to make a few criss-cross stitches just inside the raspberry – this will close in the stuffing and gather the top slightly. Decorate with pink seed beads. Sew up the side seam of each strawberry in the same way. Stuff completely, then gather the top and secure with a few stitches. Decorate with red seed beads. To finish a berry, gather up the knitted circle and secure the thread. Stitch five or six berries together to make a bunch. Secure the long thread in the middle of the tart case with a few stitches. Stretch the tart case over the jar lid. Lay a small amount of toy stuffing in the case then spread the knitted cream over the top, securing it at the edges with a few stitches. Arrange the fruit and secure through the cream with a few neat stitches.

Jazzy Cake

Materials:

1 ball pure merino wool – off-white

1 ball double knitting – multi-coloured

Small amount of decorative, multi-coloured yarn

Small amount of fluffy polyester yarn – cream

Multi-coloured seed beads

Multi-coloured bugle beads

10mm (½in) multi-coloured ribbon, 36cm (14¼in)

Toy stuffing

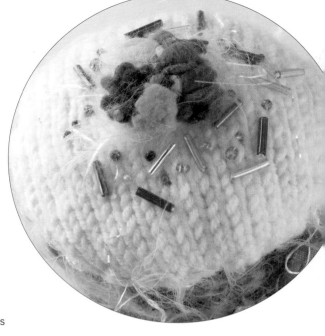

Needles:

1 pair 3.25mm (UK 10; US 3) knitting needles

Instructions:

Iced top

Cast on 10 sts in off-white using 3.25mm needles.

Rows 1–15: work in st st, starting with a k row, increasing 1 st at beg and end of each k row [26 sts].

Row 16: purl.

Row 17: knit.

Row 18: purl.

Rows 19–33: continue in st st, decreasing 1 st at beg and end of each k row [10 sts].

Row 34: purl.

Cast off.

Side of cake

Using multi-coloured double knitting and 3.25mm needles, cast on 17 sts.

Rows 1–90: st st.

Cast off.

Base of cake

Using multi-coloured double knitting and 3.25mm needles, cast on 8 sts.

Rows 1–2: work in st st, starting with a k row.

Row 3: knit, increasing 1 st at beg and end of row [10 sts].

Row 4: purl.

Row 5: knit, increasing 1 st at beg and end of row [12 sts].

Rows 6–10: continue in st st.

Row 11: knit, decreasing 1 st at beg and end of row [10 sts].

Row 12: purl.

Row 13: knit, decreasing 1 st at beg and end of row [8 sts].

Row 14: purl.

Cast off.

Making up

Make small ridges going widthways across the side of the cake, holding them in place with rows of running stitches. Stitch the short edges of the cake side together to form a tube. Sew the cake base to one end. Fill with stuffing. Sew the iced top in place. Using the fluffy polyester yarn, make a row of running stitches around the edge of the icing. Decorate the top with multi-coloured yarn and beads. Tie a ribbon around the cake and make a small bow at the front.

Opposite:

The fun pink and green jazzy cake has a green cherry on the top, which is knitted using the holly berry pattern on page 72.

Baby Cupcake

Materials:

2 balls 4 ply – 1 pink and 1 cream

1 ball 100% cotton 4 ply – white

Pink seed beads

Cardboard for base, 45mm (1¾in) diameter

Stiff, white paper

Toy stuffing

Needles:

1 pair 2.25mm (UK 13; US 1) knitting needles

Set of four 3.25mm (UK 10; US 3) double-
  pointed knitting needles

Instructions:

Top of cake

Cast on 42 sts using cream wool and double-
ended needles – 14 sts on each of 3 needles.
Rounds 1–5: knit.
Round 6: change to pink and work a k row.
Round 7: (k5, k2tog, k5, k2tog) on each needle
[12 sts on each needle].
Round 8: knit.
Round 9: (k4, k2tog, k4, k2tog) on each needle
[10 sts on each needle].
Round 10: knit.
Round 11: (k3, k2tog, k3, k2tog) on each
needle [8 sts on each needle].
Round 12: knit.
Round 13: (k2, k2tog, k2, k2tog) on each
needle [6 sts on each needle].
Round 14: knit.
Round 15: (k1, k2tog, k1, k2tog) on each
needle [4 sts on each needle].
Round 16: knit.
Round 17: (k2tog, k2tog) on each needle [2 sts
on each needle].
Break yarn, leaving a long end. Thread through
stitches on needles and draw up tightly.

Side of case

Cast on 60 sts using white cotton 4 ply and
2.25mm needles.
Rows 1–11: k1, p1 across each row.
Row 12: inc every second p st across row.
Cast off.

Base of case

Cast on 10 sts using white cotton 4 ply and
2.25mm needles. Work in st st.
Row 1: ** purl.
Row 2: inc 1 st at beg and end of row. **
Rows 3–8: repeat from ** to ** 3 times [18 sts].
Rows 9–11: continue in st st.
Rows 12–18: dec 1 st at beg and end of every k
row [10 sts].
Row 19: purl.
Cast off.

Making up

Join the sides of the cupcake case, then stitch
the bottom in place. Pull up the thread holding
the stitches at the top of the cake, and darn
the thread in to hold it firmly in place. Using
stiff paper, cut a strip large enough to wrap
around the inside of the case. Tape the sides
together to make a paper liner that fits inside
the case – this will make the case stiffer and
stop it losing its shape. Tape the cardboard
base to the paper liner, insert into the knitted
case, then fill the case and the top of the cake
with toy stuffing. Put the top on the case and
sew them together at the edges. Sew seed
beads to the top of the cupcake.

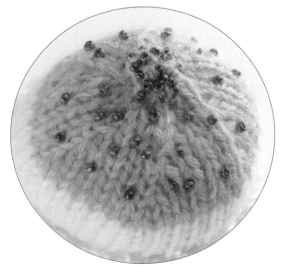

Opposite:

*The pretty baby-blue cupcake is made using
blue and white 4 ply wool. Blue seed beads
and a teddy button have been sewn to the top.*

Swiss Roll

Materials:

2 balls cotton double knitting yarn – 1 beige and 1
    raspberry

Needles:

1 pair 3.25mm (UK 10; US 3) knitting needles

Instructions:

Outer layer
Using beige cotton, cast on 20 sts.
Rows 1–60: st st.
Cast off.

Inner layer
Using raspberry cotton, cast on 20 sts.
Rows 1–50: st st.
Cast off.

Making up
With the smaller rectangle on top and
the two short edges together, roll up
the two layers tightly and evenly to
form a Swiss roll. Turn under the
end of the outer knitted layer
and stitch in place.

Opposite:
*The chocolate Swiss roll is made using
chocolate and cream double knitting wool.*

Christmas Holly Cake

Materials:

1 ball double knitting – white

Small amount of green and red double knitting

18mm (¾in) Christmas ribbon, 25cm (9¾in)

Toy stuffing

Needles:

1 pair 2.5mm (UK 12; US 2) knitting needles

1 pair 3.25mm (UK 10, US 3) knitting needles

Set of four 2.5mm (UK 12; US 2) double-
    pointed knitting needles

Instructions:

Top of cake

Cast on 51 sts using white wool and double-
ended needles – 17 sts on each of 3 needles.
Rounds 1–26: knit.
Round 27: * dec 2 sts randomly on each needle
* [15 sts on each needle].
Rounds 28–33: repeat from * to * [3 sts on each
needle].
Round 34: k2tog, k1 [2 sts on each needle].
Break yarn, leaving a long end. Thread through
stitches on needles and draw up tightly.

Base of cake

Cast on 12 sts using white wool and 2.5mm
needles and work in st st.
Row 1: ** purl.
Row 2: knit, increasing 1 st at beg and end of
row. **
Rows 3–8: repeat from ** to ** [20 sts].
Rows 9–11: continue in st st.
Rows 12–18: dec 1 st at beg and end of every k
row [12 sts].
Row 19: purl.
Cast off.

Holly

Make two leaves.

Cast on 2 sts using green wool and
3.25mm needles.
Rows 1–2: work in st st, starting with a k row.
Row 3: inc both sts [4 sts].
Rows 4–6: st st.

Row 7: inc first and last st [6 sts].
Row 8: purl.
Row 9: inc first and last st [8 sts].
Row 10: purl.
Row 11: k2tog at beg and end of row [6 sts].
Row 12: purl.
Row 13: repeat row 11 [4 sts].
Row 14: purl.
Row 15: k2tog, k2tog.
Row 16: p2tog.

Berries

Make three berries.

Cast on 5 sts using red wool and
3.25mm needles.
Rows 1–5: st st.
Cast off.

Making up

Pull up the thread at the top of the cake
holding the remaining stitches, then darn the
thread end into the stitches at the back of the
knitting. Stuff the domed cake with toy stuffing
then stitch it on to the cake base. Wrap a
length of ribbon around the cake, overlapping
the ends before stitching it in place. Make a
row of gathering stitching around the edge of
the knitted berry. Add a small amount of toy
stuffing to the centre, then pull up the thread
and secure. Stitch the holly leaves and the
berries to the top of the cake.

The holly and berries have been replaced by a charming Christmas rose on this alternative version of the domed Christmas holly cake. The rose is knitted using the flower pattern on page 88. Follow the instructions until row 7 [64 sts], then cast off in purl. Small holly-shaped beads have been used to decorate the cake.

Muffin

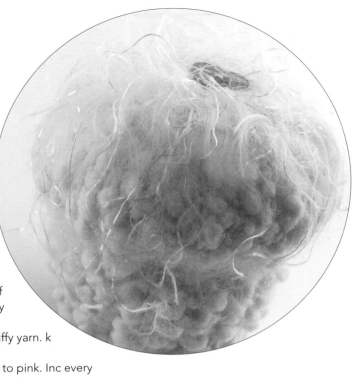

Materials:

1 ball bobbly nylon double knitting –
   pink
1 ball fluffy polyester yarn – cream
Toy stuffing
Heart-shaped button

Needles:

1 pair 3.25mm (UK 10; US 3)
   knitting needles

Instructions:

Cast on 35 sts in pink. Work in g st.
Rows 1–17: inc 1 st at beg and end of
row 2, and then beg and end of every
third row [47 sts].
Row 18: break yarn and change to fluffy yarn. k
to end of row.
Row 19: break yarn and change back to pink. Inc every
third st across row [62 sts].
Rows 20–23: change to st st, starting with a k row.
Row 24: * knit every fifth and sixth sts together across row * [52 sts].
Rows 25–27: st st.
Row 28: repeat from * to * [44 sts].
Row 29: purl.
Row 30: repeat from * to * [37 sts].
Rows 31–32: change to fluffy yarn and work in g st.
Row 33: repeat from * to * [31 sts].
Row 34: repeat from * to * [26 sts].
Row 35: knit.
Break yarn, leaving a long end. Thread through stitches on needle,
draw up tightly and fasten off.

Making up

With wrong sides facing, sew up the side seam of the muffin. Turn
right-side out. Stuff the bottom half of the muffin lightly – do
not put stuffing in the top or you will not achieve a good muffin
shape. Gather up the bottom, and secure the thread. Make rows of
running stitches around the top edge of the muffin base, just under
the row of fluffy yarn, and pull up lightly – this will help to shape
the bottom of the muffin. Pull the top into shape over the base and
stitch a heart-shaped button to the top.

Opposite:
*The chocolate muffin has
been knitted in dark brown
yarn to create a cake that
really does look good
enough to eat. The cherry
is knitted in red yarn and
covered in red seed beads
using the berry instructions
on page 64.*

Lemon Meringue

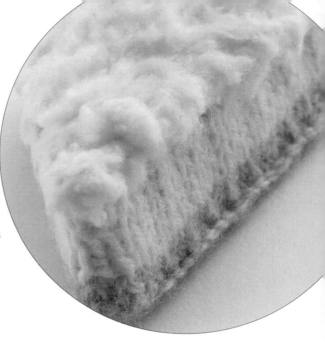

Materials:

2 balls double knitting – 1 beige and 1
  yellow

1 chunky snowflake yarn – white

Cardboard for insert, 9 x 12cm (3½ x 4¾in)

Toy stuffing

Brown felt-tipped pen

Needles:

1 pair 3.25mm (UK 10; US 3) knitting needles

Instructions:

Base and back of pastry case

Cast on 14 sts in beige.

Rows 1–6: work in st st, starting with a k row.

Row 7: purl across a k row.

Rows 8–12: work in st st, starting with a p row.

Row 13: k1, k2tog, k to last 3 sts, k2tog, k1
[12 sts].

Rows 14–16: work in st st, starting with a p row.

Row 17: k1, k2tog, k to last 3 sts, k2tog, k1
[10 sts].

Rows 18–20: work in st st, starting with a p row.

Row 21: k1, k2tog, k to last 3 sts, k2tog, k1
[8 sts].

Rows 22–24: work in st st, starting with a p row.

Row 25: k1, k2tog, k to last 3 sts, k2tog, k1
[6 sts].

Rows 26–28: work in st st, starting with a p row.

Row 29: k1, k2tog, k2tog, k1.

Row 30: purl.

Row 31: k2tog, k2tog.

Row 32: purl.

Row 33: k2tog.

Break yarn, leaving a long end. Thread through
last stitch on needle.

Sides of pastry case and filling

Pick up and knit 25 sts in beige along one
edge of the triangular pastry case base.

Row 2: purl.

Rows 3–7: change to yellow and work in st st
for 5 rows.

Cast off on a p row. Repeat for the other side
of the pastry case.

Pastry crust

The crust along the top edge of the back of the
slice is made using the instructions for piped
cream on page 58. Using beige wool, make a
row of 3 swirls.

Meringue topping

Pick up and knit 14 sts in white along the top
edge of the back of the slice.

Rows 2–4: work in st st, starting with a p row.

Row 5: *k1, k2tog, k to last 3 sts, k2tog, k1*
[12 sts].

Rows 6–8: work in st st, starting with a p row.

Row 9: repeat from * to * [10 sts].

Rows 10–12: work in st st, starting with a p row.

Row 13: repeat from * to * [8 sts].

Rows 14–16: work in st st, starting with a p row.

Row 17: repeat from * to * [6 sts].

Rows 18–20: work in st st, starting with a p row.

Row 21: k1, k2tog, k2tog, K1 [4 sts].

Row 22: purl.

Row 23: k2tog, k2tog [2 sts].

Row 24: k2tog.

Break yarn, leaving a long end. Thread through
last stitch on needle.

Opposite:

*Try knitting the chocolate version of the
meringue slice – just replace the lemon
wool with chocolate.*

Making up

On the wrong side of the knitting, stitch the sides of the pastry case to the back, and stitch the front edges together to form a point. Fold a strip of cardboard into a triangular shape to line the sides and back of the slice. It is important to make the cardboard shape slightly larger than the knitting, so that the knitting can be stretched over it. This will give a neater finish. Insert the cardboard into the slice, and fill with toy stuffing. Stretch the meringue over the top of the slice and stitch it to the filling. Sew the pastry crust to the back of the slice. Use a brown felt-tipped pen to colour the meringue to give it a cooked appearance.

Carrot Cake

Materials:

2 balls double knitting – 1 flecked cream and 1 beige

1 ball bobbly nylon double knitting – off-white

Small amount of double knitting in orange and green

Brown, walnut, peach and cream seed beads

Cardboard for insert, 8 x 25cm (3¼ x 9¾in)

Toy stuffing

Needles:

1 pair 3.25mm (UK 10; US 3) knitting needles

Instructions:

Follow the instructions for the Chocolate Gateau on page 58. The top of the cake is knitted in bobbly double knitting, the back and base in flecked double knitting with the centre layer in beige. Knit two rows of 3 piped cream swirls for the back of the cake in off-white bobbly wool.

Carrot

Cast on 10 sts in orange.

Row 1: knit.
Row 2: purl.
Row 3: (k1, k2tog) 3 times, k1 [7 sts].
Row 4: purl.
Row 5: (k1, k2tog) twice, k1 [5 sts].
Row 6: purl.
Row 7: knit.
Row 8: purl.
Row 9: k1, k2tog, k1.
Row 10: p3tog.

Break yarn and thread through last stitch on the needle.

Carrot top

Cast on 2 sts using green wool.
Rows 1–2: g st.
Cast off.

Making up

The carrot cake is assembled in the same way as the Chocolate Gateau on page 58. Stitch the two lengths of piped cream swirls to the cake. Decorate the cake by randomly stitching seed beads to the back. Stitch the carrot top to the carrot, and then sew it to the top of the cake.

Viennese Whirl

Materials:

1 ball 4 ply – cream

1 ball fluffy mohair acrylic mix – cream

Small amount of red double knitting

Toy stuffing

Brown felt-tipped pen

Needles:

1 pair 3.25mm (UK 10; US 3) knitting needles

Set of four 2.5mm (UK 12; US 2) double-
  pointed knitting needles

Instructions:

Whirl

For each cake, make four circular whirls.

Cast on 60 sts using cream wool and double-
ended needles – 20 sts on each of 3 needles.
Rounds 1–3: knit.
Round 4: knit, decreasing first and last st on
each needle [18 sts on each needle].
Round 5: purl, decreasing first and last st on
each needle [16 sts on each needle].
Round 6: repeat round 5 [14 sts on
each needle].
Round 7: repeat round 4 [12 sts on
each needle].
Round 8: repeat round 4 [10 sts on
each needle].
Round 9: repeat round 5 [8 sts on each needle].

Round 10: repeat round 5 [6 sts on
each needle].
Round 11: repeat round 4 [4 sts on
each needle].
Round 12: k2tog, k2tog on each needle [2 sts
on each needle].
Round 13: k2tog on each needle [1 st on
each needle].
Break yarn, leaving a long end. Thread through
stitches on needle and draw up tightly.

Cream

Cast on 10 sts in fluffy mohair acrylic using
3.25mm needles and work in g st.
Row 1: knit.
Row 2: inc 1 st at beg and end of row [12 sts].
Row 3: knit.
Row 4: inc 1 st at beg and end of row [14 sts].
Rows 5–16: st st, starting with a k row.
Row 17: k2tog at beg and end of row [12 sts].
Row 18: knit.
Row 19: k2tog at beg and end of row [10 sts].
Row 20: knit.
Cast off.

Cherry

Cast on 5 sts in red wool using 3.25mm
needles.
Rows 1–4: st st.
Cast off.

Making up

Pull up the thread holding the stitches at the
top of the whirl, and darn the thread end
into the stitches to hold them firmly in place.
With wrong sides together, place two whirls
together, lightly stuff, then over-stitch the
edges. Repeat with the other two whirls. Make
a row of running stitches around the edge of
the cream then pull up the thread to gather
it slightly. Sew the two completed halves of
the Viennese whirl together with the cream
layer between them. Make a row of gathering
stitching around the edge of the knitted cherry.
Add a small amount of toy stuffing to the
centre, then pull up the thread and secure. Sew
the cherry on to the centre top. Use a brown
felt-tipped pen to add a few flecks of colour to
the edges and top of the whirl.

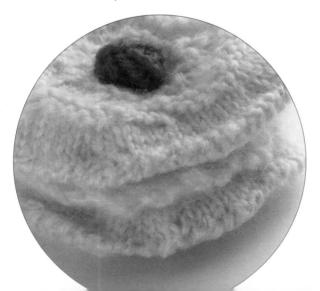

Raspberry Heart Cake

Materials:

2 balls double knitting – 1 flecked pink and
   1 maroon

Small amount of fluffy polyester yarn – cream

Pink ribbon rose

Toy stuffing

Needles:

1 pair 3.25mm (UK 10; US 3) knitting needles

Stitch holder

Instructions:

Top and base of heart

Knit one heart in flecked pink double knitting
and one in maroon double knitting.

Cast on 2 sts.
Rows 1–2: st st, starting with a k row.
Row 3: knit, increasing 1 st at beg and end of
row [4 sts].
Row 4: purl.
Row 5: repeat row 3 [6 sts].
Row 6: purl.
Row 7: repeat row 3 [8 sts].
Row 8: purl.
Row 9: repeat row 3 [10 sts].
Row 10: purl.
Row 11: repeat row 3 [12 sts].
Rows 12–14: continue in st st.
Row 15: knit, increasing 1 st at beg and end of
row [14 sts].
Rows 16–18: continue in st st.
Row 19: repeat row 15 [16 sts].
Row 20: p first 8 sts. Turn and continue
working on these 8 sts. Transfer other sts to
stitch holder.
Row 21: *k2tog, k4, k2tog.
Row 22: purl.
Row 23: k2tog, k2, k2tog.
Row 24: purl.
Row 25: k2tog, k2tog.
Row 26: p2tog.

Break yarn, leaving a long end. Thread through
last stitch on needle.*
Transfer 8 sts on stitch holder to needle and
repeat from * to * .

Side of heart

Cast on 10 sts.
Rows 1–75: st st.
Cast off.

Making up

With wrong sides facing, sew the short edges
of the side strip together. Stitch the heart-
shaped top to the side, easing it gently into
shape. Repeat for the base, leaving a small
gap for stuffing. Turn right-side out and fill with
toy stuffing. Stitch up the gap. Stitch a circle of
white fluffy yarn to the top of the heart with the
ribbon rose in the centre.

Opposite:

*The side and base of the alternative version
of this cake have been knitted using pink
double knitting wool. The raspberries are
made using the pattern on page 65.*

Cherry Pie Slice

Materials:

2 balls wool-cotton double knitting – 1 cream and 1 raspberry

Cherry red chunky beads

Cherry red seed beads

Cardboard for base, 7 x 10cm (2¾ x 4in)

Toy stuffing

Needles:

1 pair 3.25mm (UK 10; US 3) knitting needles

Instructions:

Cherry filling

Cast on 18 sts.

Row 1: (right side) purl.

Row 2: k1, *(k1, p1, k1) into next st, p3tog.*
Repeat from * to * to last st, k1.

Row 3: purl.

Row 4: k1, **p3tog, (k1, p1, k1) into next st.**
Repeat from ** to ** to last st, k1.

Row 5: purl.

Row 6: repeat row 2.

Row 7: purl.

Row 8: k1, repeat from ** to ** 3 times, p3tog, k2 [16 sts].

Row 9: purl.

Row 10: k1, repeat from * to * 3 times, (k1, p1, k1) into next st, k2tog [17 sts].

Row 11: p2tog, p to last 4 sts, p2tog, p2tog [14 sts].

Row 12: k2, repeat from * to * 3 times.

Row 13: purl.

Row 14: k1, repeat from * to * 3 times, k1.

Row 15: p2tog, p to last 2 sts, p2tog [12 sts].

Row 16: Repeat from ** to ** twice, p3tog, k1 [10 sts].

Row 17: purl.

Row 18: k1, repeat from ** to ** twice, k1.

Row 19: purl.

Row 20: k1, repeat from * to * twice, k1.

Row 21: purl.

Row 22: k1, repeat from * to * twice, k1 [10 sts].

Row 23: purl.

Row 24: p4tog, repeat from * to * once, (k1, p1, k1) into next st, k1 [9 sts].

Row 25: purl.

Row 26: p4tog, repeat from * to * once, k1 [6 sts].

Row 27: p3tog, p3tog.

Row 28: p2tog.

Cast off.

Base and back of pastry case

Cast on 14 sts in cream.

Rows 1–6: st st, starting with a k row.

Row 7: purl across a k row.

Rows 8–12: work in st st, starting with a p row.

Row 13: k1, k2tog, k to last 3 sts, k2tog, k1 [12 sts].

Rows 14–16: work in st st, starting with a p row.

Row 17: k1, k2tog, k to last 3 sts, k2tog, k1 [10 sts].

Rows 18–20: work in st st, starting with a p row.

Row 21: k1, k2tog, k to last 3 sts, k2tog, k1 [8 sts].

Rows 22–24: work in st st, starting with a p row.

Row 25: k1, k2tog, k to last 3 sts, k2tog, k1 [6 sts].

Rows 26–28: work in st st, starting with a p row.

Row 29: k1, k2tog, k2tog, k1.

Row 30: purl.

Row 31: k2tog, k2tog.

Row 32: purl.

Row 33: k2tog.

Break yarn, leaving a long end. Thread through last stitch on needle.

Sides of pastry case

With right sides facing, pick up and knit 22 sts from one long side of the triangular base.

Rows 1–6: work in st st, starting with a p row.

Cast off.

Repeat for the other side.

Pastry crust

The crust along the top edge of the back of the slice is made using the instructions for piped cream on page 58. Using cream wool, make a row of 4 swirls.

Cream blob

Cast on 8 sts and work in g st.

Row 1: * knit.

Row 2: knit, increasing 1 st at beg and end of row * [10 sts].

Rows 3–8: repeat from * to * until 16 sts remain.

Rows 9–11: knit.

Row 12: ** dec 1 st at beg and end of row [14 sts].

Row 13: knit. **

Rows 14–17: repeat from ** to ** twice [10 sts].

Row 18: repeat row 12 [8 sts].

Cast off.

Making up

With wrong sides facing, sew up the front and back seams of the tart case. Cut a cardboard triangle to fit inside the case. Place it in the bottom and stuff with toy stuffing. Place the knitted cherry filling over the stuffing and stitch to the case. Stitch the pastry crust to the back of the case. To make the cream blob, fold the knitted shape in half lengthways and stitch along the edge. Re-shape the knitting so that the seam runs down the centre, then roll it up and secure with a few stitches. Attach the cream to the cherry filling. Sew beads to the top of the pie.

Plum is the flavour of this alternative pie slice, with the filling stitched using mauve wool-cotton mix. Bugle beads and a blob of cream complete this dessert.

Crazy Cupcake

Materials:

1 ball big pin knitting yarn – red
1 ball metallic knitting yarn – gold
Cardboard for base, 45mm (1¾in) diameter
Stiff, white paper, 4 x 13cm (1½ x 5in)
Toy stuffing

Needles:

1 pair 4mm (UK 8; US 6) knitting needles
1 pair 3.25mm (UK 10; US 3) knitting needles

Instructions:

Top of cupcake

Using 4mm needles and big pin knitting yarn, cast on 25 sts. Work in g st.
Rows 1–9: knit.
Row 10: *k4, k2tog.* Repeat from * to * to last st, k1 [21 sts].
Row 11: knit.
Row 12: **k3, k2tog.** Repeat from ** to ** to last st, k1 [17 sts].
Row 13: knit.
Break yarn, leaving a long end. Thread through stitches on needle and draw up tightly.

Cupcake case

Using metallic thread and 3.25mm needles, cast on 48 sts. Work in rib.
Rows 1–11: (k1, p1) to end.
Row 12: (k1, p1) to end, increasing every second p st.
Cast off.

Case base

Using metallic thread and 3.25mm needles, cast on 8 sts.
Row 1: purl.
Row 2: knit, increasing at beg and end of row [10 sts].
Rows 3–6: repeat rows 1 and 2 twice [14 sts].
Row 7: purl.
Row 8: knit.
Row 9: purl.
Row 10: knit, decreasing at beg and end of row [12 sts].
Row 11–14: repeat rows 9 and 10 twice [8 sts].
Cast off.

Making up

With wrong sides facing, sew up the side seam of the cupcake top. Turn right-side out. Pull up the thread holding the stitches at the top of the cake, and darn the thread end in to hold it firmly in place. With wrong sides facing, sew up the side seam of the cupcake case. Turn right-side out. Stitch the base to the side of the cake. Using stiff paper, cut a strip large enough to wrap around the inside of the case. Tape the sides together to make a paper liner that will fit inside the case – this will make the case stiffer and stop it losing its shape. Tape the cardboard base to the paper liner, insert it in the knitted case, then fill the case and the top of the cake with toy stuffing. Stitch the top to the bottom at the edges.

Opposite:

The blue version of the Crazy Cupcake is simple to knit in just a couple of hours. The top is knitted using blue big pin knitting yarn and the case is in silver metallic thread.

Angel Cake

Materials:

2 balls 4 ply – 1 pink and 1 pale pink
Short lengths of green wool for leaves
Cardboard for insert, 6 x 20cm (2¼ x 7¾in)
Toy stuffing

Needles:

1 pair 3.25mm (UK 10; US 3) knitting needles

Instructions:

Sides of cake

Cast on 60 sts in pink wool. Work in g st.
Rows 1–5: knit.
Rows 6–7: change to pale pink and work in st st, starting with a k row.
Rows 8–9: change back to pink and continue in st st.
Rows 10–11: change to pale pink and continue in st st.
Rows 12–13: change to pink and continue in st st.
Rows 14–15: change to pale pink and continue in st st.
Rows 16–21: change to pink and work in g st.
Cast off.

Top and bottom of cake

Cast on 14 sts.
Rows 1–21: st st.
Cast off.

Flower

Cast on 8 sts using pink. Work in st st.
Row 1: knit.
Row 2: purl.
Row 3: knit, increasing every st [16 sts].
Row 4: purl.
Row 5: knit, increasing every st [32 sts].
Row 6: purl.
Row 7: knit, increasing every st [64 sts].
Row 8: purl.
Row 9: knit, increasing every fourth st across row [80 sts].
Cast off.

Leaves

Cast on 2 sts and work in g st.
Row 1: knit.
Row 2: * inc every st * [4 sts].
Rows 3–4: knit.
Row 5: repeat from * to * [6 sts].
Rows 6–7: knit.
Row 8: k2tog at beg and end of row [4 sts].
Rows 9–10: knit.
Row 11: k2tog, k2tog [2 sts].
Row 12: k2tog.
Break yarn and pull through last stitch.

Making up

Join together the two short edges of the cake side to make a tube. Working on the right side of the knitting, use small running stitches to attach the cake base to the side – working on the right side will make a ridge on the edge of the cake. Roll the cardboard into a flattened tube shape, overlapping the ends, insert it into the cake and stuff. Sew the top on the cake in the same way as the base. Roll the flower up into a pleasing shape and secure it with a few stitches. Attach the flower and the leaves to the top of the cake.

Opposite:

This delicious chocolate version of the angel cake is made using dark brown and cream 4 ply wool.

Materials:

4 balls double knitting – 1 white, 1 peach,
  1 dark brown and 1 brown
1 ball cotton double knitting – orange
Gold embroidery thread
Pearl beads
Cardboard for lining, 8 x 30cm (3¼ x 11¾in)
Toy stuffing

Needles:

1 pair 3.25mm (UK 10; US 3) knitting needles

Instructions:

The back, top and base of the cake are knitted
in one piece using white double knitting and
3.25mm needles. The instructions are the same
as for the Chocolate Gateau on page 58.

Sides of cake

Fold the knitted back, top and base so that you
can see which of the two triangular sections will
be the top of your cake. You will be knitting the
side of the cake from the iced top down.
Row 1: with right side facing, pick up and knit 24
sts in white along one side of the
triangular top.
Row 2: purl.
Row 3: change to orange and k to end of row.
Row 4: purl.
Row 5: knit.
Rows 6–24: work in st st using two shades of
brown, starting with a p row. Change colour
randomly across each row to get a mottled fruit
cake effect. Take care to keep tension even as
wool is taken across back of work.
Cast off.
Repeat for other side of cake.

Marzipan on back of cake

Row 1: with right side facing, pick up and knit 24
sts in white down one side of the cake back.
Row 2: purl.
Row 3: change to orange and k to end of row.
Row 4: purl.
Cast off.
Repeat for the other side.

Peach icing balls

Make six individual balls of peach icing – three
for the iced edging along the top of the cake
and three for the base (not shown).
Cast on 2 sts. Work g st for 5 rows. Cast off.

Royal icing

Using the piped cream instructions on page 58,
make two lengths of 4 icing swirls.

Making up

With wrong sides facing, sew the cake sides
together along the front edge. Turn right-side
out. Cut and fold the strip of cardboard into
a triangular shape to fit inside the cake – the
top and bottom are left unlined. It is important
to make the cardboard shape slightly larger
than the knitting, so that the knitting can be
stretched when sewn into place. Line the
cake and fill it with toy stuffing. Sew the cake
sides to the base of the cake. Repeat for the
other side. Ease the marzipan attached to the
back of the cake just under the cake sides
and carefully stitch it in place. Sew the two
Royal icing strips to the back of the cake – one
along the top and one along the base. Sew
the peach icing balls between the Royal icing
swirls. Using gold embroidery thread, stitch a
criss-cross pattern on the back and top of the
cake. Sew pearl beads at the intersections.

Cupcake Egg Cosy

Materials:

2 balls pure merino – 1 chocolate and 1 pink

1 ball 100% cotton 4 ply – white

Short lengths of pure merino wool in lime green for the embroidery

Needles:

1 pair 2.75mm (UK 12; US 2) knitting needles

1 pair 2.25mm (UK 13; US 1) knitting needles

Instructions:

Top of cupcake

Cast on 36 sts in brown wool using 2.75mm needles.

Rows 1–6: st st.

Rows 7–18: change to pink and work in g st.

Row 19: knit, decreasing 4 sts randomly across row [32 sts].

Row 20: knit.

Row 21: knit, decreasing 4 sts randomly across row [28 sts].

Row 22: knit.

Row 23: knit, decreasing 4 sts randomly across row [24 sts].

Row 24: knit.

Row 25: knit, decreasing 4 sts randomly across row [20 sts].

Row 26: knit.

Break yarn, leaving a long end. Thread through stitches on needle and draw up tightly.

Side of case

Cast on 60 sts using white cotton 4 ply and 2.25mm needles.

Rows 1–11: (k1, p1) to end of row.

Row 12: inc every second p st across row.

Cast off.

Making up

Join the two sides of the case and the cupcake top. Pull up the thread holding the stitches at the top of the cake, and darn the thread end in to hold it firmly in place. Stitch the case to the cake top. Using lime green wool, work sets of four lazy daisy stitches randomly over the top of the cake. If you enjoy a larger breakfast egg, knit the cosy using larger needles!

Opposite:

Why not make a complete set of these stylish egg cosies to match your own kitchen? This alternative design has been made using blue and cream wool and has dark blue lazy daisy stitches embroidered on.

Fruit Fancy

Materials:

3 balls double knitting – 1 lemon, 1 yellow and 1 white

Small amount of green, mauve and orange wool

Black seed beads

Cardboard for insert, 6 x 44cm (2¼ x 17¼in)

Toy stuffing

Needles:

1 pair 3.25mm (UK 10; US 3) knitting needles

Instructions:

Base and top of cake

Make two diamond shapes, one in yellow and one in lemon, for the base and top of the cake.

Cast on 2 sts in yellow or lemon wool.

Rows 1–2: st st, starting with a k row.

Rows 3–14: inc 1 st at beg of every row until 14 sts remain.

Row 15: knit.

Rows 16–27: dec 1 st at beg of every row until 2 sts remain.

Rows 28–29: st st.

Cast off.

Sides of cake

Cast on 60 sts in lemon.

Rows 1–8: st st.

Rows 9–10: change to white and work 2 rows in st st.

Rows 11–17: change back to lemon and work 7 rows in st st.

Rows 18–19: change to yellow and work 2 rows in st st.

Cast off.

Fruit

The fruit is made using the instructions for the fruit tart on page 64. You will need to make one slice of kiwi, three berries and one slice of orange.

Making up

Sew the short edges of the cake side together. Pin the assembled side to the cake base, and at each point of the diamond make a seam on the cake side, working on the wrong side of the knitting, from top to bottom – this will help the cake keep its diamond shape when stuffed. Sew the side of the cake to the base, lining up the seams and the diamond points. Cut a strip of cardboard the same height as the cake, and long enough to fit round the inside of the cake with a small overlap. Bend the cardboard into a diamond shape and insert it into the cake. Fill with toy stuffing, and then attach the top. Sew the fruit to the top of the cake.

Opposite:

The pretty strawberry version of the fruit fancy is made using cream and pink double knitting wool. Lemon slices, berries and a raspberry have been sewn to the top – see the instructions on pages 64 and 65.

Publishers' Note
If you would like more books about novelty knitting, try *Knitted Flowers* by Susie Johns,
Search Press 2009; and *Knitted Bears* by Val Pierce, Search Press 2009; both from the
Twenty to Make series.

If you would like more information on knitting techniques, try the
Beginner's Guide to Knitting by Alison Dupernex, Search Press, 2004; and the
Compendium of Knitting Techniques by Betty Barnden, Search Press, 2008.